The Las Vegas Experts' Gambling Guide

The
Las Vegas
Experts'
GAMBLING
GUIDE

♠

by

ROBERT SCHARFF

Publishers / GROSSET & DUNLAP / New York

Contents

The Las Vegas Experts' Gambling Guide

Gambling Las Vegas Style

The world-famous city of Las Vegas, Nevada, is variously known as the Monte Carlo of North America, the Crossroads of Scenic America, and the Gateway to Western Wonderland. Regardless of which of these names you choose, none could fully describe the wonders and electric excitement of this fabulous resort. Sprung from the bosom of the sun-drenched desert, nurtured by the Nevada law legalizing gambling in all its forms, publicized and promoted the world over through its development as the capital of the entertainment world, Las Vegas and the word fabulous have become synonymous. Here has mushroomed the largest and most lavish of the world's spectacular resort hotels, offering the biggest and best of the world's entertainers in the fantastic atmosphere of luxury, excitement and "twenty-four hour action."

Gambling and Las Vegas

As everyone in the world must have heard by now, there is a great deal of gambling going on in Las Vegas. Gambling is legal there, as it is in the rest of the state, and undoubtedly accounts for the fact that Vegas resorts are always so crowded. Without Craps, Roulette, Twenty-One (Blackjack), Keno and the rest, the resorts would be unable to offer the fine food and entertainment they do for such paltry prices.

People who have qualms about gambling can easily ignore the

sport. Many do—particularly Nevadans who have lived with it for so many decades they take it for granted. But if they want to, people can gamble in Nevada freely and legally, secure in the knowledge that this is a state-controlled industry, carefully regulated and inspected, and aboveboard in every respect. Many other states, of course, allow games of chance. Twenty-four, in fact, have legalized gambling in one form or another—horse racing, for example—and six of these states take in more in tax revenues from gambling than Nevada does. The unique thing about Las Vegas is there is no *illegal* gambling there.

Behind all its rich façade, gambling in Nevada operates on sound business principles. And it owes its existence to a tradition of liberal attitudes of the people. Gambling exists in Nevada for three primary reasons:

1. It has been an economic success, both from the standpoint of its effect on general business, and from tax revenue.

2. Because of its small population, Nevada is perhaps the only state in which gambling is relatively easy to control.

3. The liberal attitude of the people still prevails.

This attitude of liberality is not difficult to understand. From territorial days, gambling has flourished in this frontier state with few problems. No town was complete without its casinos, and the Faro dealer was an integral part of the Nevada scene. Gambling became big business when tourism came of age. It was inevitable that the attraction of open gambling would make Nevada a "must stop" in this ever-growing westward movement. Casinos began to enlarge and multiply. Luxury hotels with elaborate theatre-restaurants and swimming pools sprang up almost overnight in Las Vegas. Population soared and the number of businesses doubled and then tripled. Tourism had suddenly become an indispensable part of the state's economy. Today, more than fifteen million tourists from all parts of the United States and many foreign countries trek to Las Vegas each year. They come to visit the casinos and the luxury hotels and motels, and to see the brightest names on the nation's entertainment circuit.

As stated previously, gambling is controlled and policed by the State of Nevada. In 1945, the legislature delegated licensing power to the Nevada Tax Commission. And in 1955, the legislature created a three-man Gaming Control Board under the Tax Commission, empowering it to screen all applicants for licenses, investigate their backgrounds, police casinos for infractions of gaming regulations and to recommend approval or denial of any license application. In 1959, the State Legislature created a five-man Nevada Gaming Commission to function as the ultimate authority on regulation of gaming. The commission is charged with keeping the industry honest and insuring the state its proper tax from the gaming industry. The State Gaming Control Board was made the enforcement division of the Gaming Commission, with the same powers it held under the Tax Commission. Board investigators are all former law enforcement officers, most of them with FBI training. Actually, there is three-way supervision of gambling in Las Vegas. City and county boards have entirely independent licensing and control over gaming in their jurisdiction, although they cannot take action on a licensing application until the Nevada Gaming Commission has approved it.

Las Vegas' casinos offer several kinds of gaming. Of prime importance to the "house" and most popular with players are Blackjack, or Twenty-One, Craps and Roulette. Add to this the lesser known games of Baccarat, Pan, Poker, Faro, Keno and side games of Bingo, Wheel of Fortune, and Big Six. The greatest amount of play, of course, comes from the slot machine, affectionately called the "one-armed bandit." The "slot" requires no talent, knowledge, or skill, and simply requires the player to insert a coin and pull a handle. Some innovations to appear on the scene lately have even refined the process to the point that one need not even pull the handle . . . it is done electronically. But this, it was soon discovered, lost popularity because the player seemed to want to "do" some part of the game. Whether his method of pulling the handle ever effected the way the reels stopped is a matter of conjecture.

The gambler has two gambling areas to choose from in Las Vegas. One is the downtown section, a glittering neon kaleidoscope sometimes called the "Times Square of the West," but more generally known as "Casino Center." Concentrated in just a two-block section are twelve hotels and casinos standing wall to wall. Here is the home of the penny slot, the 10 cent Roulette chip, the

25 cent Craps table and the Bingo games. With neither doors nor windows to obstruct the view of the passer-by, these so-called "sawdust joints" candidly display their *raison d'être*, the slot machine, row upon row. Following the slots in popularity in Casino Center are Craps, Blackjack, Keno and Roulette.

The other area is the fabulous "Strip." This is actually a strip, running approximately three and one-half miles south from the Las Vegas city-county line. The Strip houses eighteen major hotel-casinos, or "carpet joints." The most obvious gambling difference found in the Strip casinos, when compared with those downtown, is the accentuation of the bigger games. While slot machines are in evidence, the major action is at Craps, Blackjack and Roulette. The minimum wager at a Strip casino is usually $1, while 25 cent bets are possible downtown. Limits—the maximum amount any player can bet at one time—are generally higher, too.

Among the pleasures of gambling, certainly the greatest is winning. Anyone who has ever had a $1 bet pay off or the contents of the pot shoved his way, knows the special exaltation that comes from a combination of pride in skill and joy at the sense of accomplishment. The moral issue is neither here nor there. People will gamble, come what may; actually, gambling—legal and illegal —has grown to where it is at the top of the industrial list. It has been estimated that revenue from gambling in the United States is greater than the combined revenue of the nation's 75 largest corporations. Gambling is here to stay in our country—despite the activities of do-gooders, religious groups and vote-seeking politicians—but it is only completely legal in Nevada.

You might ask, why should the casinos of America's gambling capital divulge their "secrets" and techniques on gambling. There are four big reasons:

1. The house will always *win* in the long run. As you will learn in Chapter 2, the casino has a built-in advantage which always proves itself over a period of time.

2. To put to rest some of the information in recent books by mathematicians and so-called gaming theoreticians which advise the novice how to destroy the dealer, harass the house, and clip the casino. Most of these authors fail to understand the facts of just how casinos operate. One of the most popular of these, written on

Blackjack, is based primarily on a one-player-vs.-dealer situation (head-to-head play). This is seldom possible because the Blackjack tables are filled to their full complement of six players nearly 80 per cent of the time. Thus, the techniques described in that book are almost worthless under actual casino conditions.

3. A winner is the best publicity that a casino and the city can have. When a player goes home from Vegas a winner he tells his friends, which helps to build up an interest by many people to see "the fun capital of the world." Actually, word of mouth advertising is important, since it is illegal to use the normal media to advertise gambling except in Nevada.

4. A player with a knowledge of the game speeds up play and makes it easier on the dealers and pit bosses. If you have any question about play of the game, or about the casino in general, ask the pit boss on duty. He will be glad to answer it in the best way he can.

It must be remembered that the management of a casino-hotel is well aware of the value of repeat business. They know that they must provide value for the customer's money. There is strong competition among the various Strip hotels and between the Strip operations and downtown Casino Center. One thing you will find in Vegas is that a casino treats its customers like kings.

Entertainment and Las Vegas

The "casino" is the hub and heart of all Las Vegas hotel operations. The remainder of the facilities of the establishment are designed to lure the customer and to keep his wife and family, if they have accompanied him, busy and happy. In addition, casino-hotel owners have learned through the years that the player needs a break from gambling, and that a too rapid separation from his money is "bad" for repeat business. Thus, they provide championship golf courses, elaborate swimming pools, gourmet restaurants, and spectacular entertainment. Be sure to take full advantage of the facilities offered.

For instance, on the Strip there are usually five, million-dollar extravaganzas, at least one major Broadway production on stage at all times, and six other shows starring top show business names.

Downtown, in more than a dozen clubs, shows are not only continuous, but feature fast-paced musical combos, singing groups and stage acts that go on ad infinitum. It is an undisputed fact that there are more entertainers and musicians playing before live audiences in Las Vegas than in any other city in the world.

For the once-in-a-while theatre-goer or the seldom night clubber, it is astounding to realize that each colorful musical production features a cast of approximately fifty persons. The payrolls for the dancers, showgirls, stage hands, electricians and countless professional people behind the scenes, average between $60,000 and $75,000 a week. The stage effects are astounding also, with lavishly costumed (or uncostumed) showgirls, exquisite staging and scenery, trapeze aerialists who seem to swing out over the audience from nowhere, and a constant array of special effects which set Las Vegas shows apart from the rest. If you miss one performance of your favorite comedian, chanteuse or dancer, there will always be another show in an hour or so in any of the many fine lounges. Most hotels schedule entertainment all night long, and into the wee hours.

Las Vegas does not limit its horizon on what the "jet set" might call "staid performances." Instead, it acknowledges the fact that patrons would like the continental flavor and has included international stars and performances to its savory list of talent. For the past several years Las Vegas show producers have known the importance of typically French fare to attract show-goers. Today there are three such revues, the famous French "Folies Bergere," the "Casino de Paris" and the elegant "Lido de Paris." Along with this continental flavor, it is not unusual, driving along the Strip or in downtown "Casino Center," to see the names of top Hollywood, Broadway and TV luminaries on hotel marquees. This delectable entertainment menu is subject to change on a week-to-week basis. *Show Guide*—a listing of Vegas shows—is available at all hotels at no charge.

All this wealth of entertainment is served up continuously every day of the week. The usual pattern among the showroom restaurants is to present a dinner show starting about eight P.M., then a late show about midnight. Some hotels offer "late-late" shows on

Friday and Saturday nights beginning about two A.M. There is never an admission charge or the need for tickets, but it is advisable that reservations be made as far in advance as possible, usually with a simple phone call to the office of the hotel's maître d'.

Of all the wondrous and unusual diversions for which Las Vegas has become justly famous, perhaps the most underpublicized is its fantastic array of first-class restaurants. Nearly fifty of the more than 200 restaurants in the city can be classified as true gourmet rooms, yet every appetite can be appeased whether your taste runs to hamburger, continental cuisine, groaning buffet boards or multi-course banquets.

While each major "Strip" hotel has its own version of the gourmet restaurant, all are characterized by plush decor, elegant entrees, impeccable service and quiet atmosphere. But do not let all this gourmet talk lead to the impression that Las Vegas has become nothing more than a fancy food factory.

Las Vegas enjoys ideal year-around climate. Spring and fall days are warm, with nights cool and refreshing. Average summer temperatures are in the 90's, but air-conditioning and extremely low humidity make for comfort indoors and out. And sunshine is another thing Las Vegas has in abundance, 99 out of every 100 days. It glistens constantly on hundreds of king-sized resort hotel pools, making Las Vegas something of a sunworshiper's paradise. And today, many a vacationer would no more leave home his golf clubs than his rabbit's foot. A peek down from the window of an airliner as it circles for a landing at McCarran Airport reveals why experts proclaim this area, for its size, to have the greatest concentration of championship golf courses in the world—seven to be exact. There are also several driving ranges and two nine-holers. Clubs and other equipment can be rented if you desire.

Many are surprised to discover what an outdoor-type town Las Vegas really is. Like center target, the city sits at the heart of a circle of outdoor wonders that includes Grand Canyon, Hoover Dam, Mount Charleston, Lake Mead, Bryce Canyon, Zion National Park and Valley of Fire. The latter is a colorful area about thirty-five miles northeast of Las Vegas that has petrified trees, prehistoric inscriptions and a large eroded sandstone basin.

Most hotels have health clubs with massages, steam baths, sun lamps, and many other services to keep you healthy and comfortable.

Inside Las Vegas

A successful trip to Las Vegas really begins with pre-planning before you leave home. While there are over 25,000 first-class rooms and suites available, it is wise to make accommodation reservations in advance, particularly on weekends. Complete listings of hotel and motel accommodations and current entertainment may be obtained by writing the Las Vegas Chamber of Commerce, 2301 East Sahara Avenue, Las Vegas, Nevada 89101.

Before going to Vegas you should become *thoroughly* familiar with the various games you plan to play. The word *thoroughly* cannot be overemphasized. Before anyone risked his money it would normally be assumed that he would learn about the games he plans to play. But most pit bosses assure me that all too many Las Vegas visitors make a constant repetition of the same old costly errors and mismanagement of money, plus the fact they do not attempt to correct these chronic violations of fundamental play. It just makes good sense that if a player covets any hope of winning, he should sternly adhere to proper play, consider the odds involved, and impose complete self-discipline in money management matters. Any passionate sportsman, whether he be a fisherman, golfer, hunter or yachtsman, spends a great deal of time and even money to learn his endeavor well. Thus, any would-be gambler at Las Vegas owes it to himself to play with some measure of proficiency. The by-product of your gambling venture is either gain or loss of hard-to-come-by money. The remaining chapters of this book will help you gain some proficiency in the sport of gambling. If possible, study and practice the techniques involved before your visit to Las Vegas.

Another important pre-planning detail is to set the amount of money you plan to gamble. You should carefully figure out the exact amount of money you can afford to lose and then budget that over the entire time of your stay. Generally, it is a good idea to make daily equal divisions of your gaming capital. The possible exception to this is on the first day when a half portion should be allotted. It is most important that you become acclimated to the casino environment before you gamble seriously.

This is a good rule to follow no matter how many times you visit Vegas. After checking into your room and deciding the show schedule you wish to follow, walk through the casino, carefully observing the play of all games. Then, study very intensely the game you plan to play. If you have any questions, do not be afraid or ashamed to ask casino personnel. They will answer them courteously and accurately. Most casino personnel, however, are discouraged from having personal involvement with customers.

Limit your first day's gaming activities to an hour or so at the most. The initial excitement of casino life will often affect your judgment and result in higher losses than you can really afford. Rather than starting serious gambling immediately, many expert players visit Casino Center first. Such a visit serves two purposes: 1) it allows a further acclimation to Las Vegas; and 2) it provides an initial gambling experience at lower betting levels.

If you wish, it is possible to make credit arrangements prior to arrival in Vegas. In your letter of application to the casino manager, state the credit limit desired, and give him your banking references, both checking and savings. It is not necessary to establish credit with more than one casino, since the others will exchange information and immediate credit will be granted. If you have not established credit at any casino in the area, the credit manager may well refuse to cash any checks for you until your credit references are checked. However, if your application and appearance indicate a substantial enough net worth, the credit manager may authorize credit to a maximum of $250 to $500. But, once you have established a credit limit that you wish to maintain, never try to raise it (see page 27).

Almost any mode of dress is acceptable in the casinos. Informal dress, even to the extent of Bermuda shorts, is fine for morning and afternoon play. Evening players, however, should be more formally dressed; typical restaurant attire is preferred for this session. Generally speaking, the Strip casinos call for a higher level of dress, especially in the evening, than those downtown.

Las Vegas casinos are classified as private clubs, but they are, in practice, open to the entire general adult public with a minimum age of twenty-one for both females and males. Their status of private clubs allows them to bar individuals they consider objectionable or undesirable.

There are many types of "player" in Las Vegas. Despite the distorted image projected by movie and television, exposé and fictional tales, and so-called word-of-mouth stories, the "player" of Vegas is just an average visitor or wagering tourist. A "smart" or "educated" player is one who knows the play of game, the odds and how to manage his money. The high-rollers, or "good customers," are those who spend plenty of money and receive special favors from the casinos, such as best seats at shows and free room accommodation. The latter is usually true for a good customer who has had a particularly bad trip. Remember that there is one type of player that no one wants, and he is the loud, boisterous, quarrelsome, sore loser.

The people you do business with in Law Vegas casinos, especially the employees who conduct the various games you play, form a very interesting and vital part of the whole gambling picture. How honest are they? How competent are they? How much are they paid? Do they depend on tips? How do you go about trying to get a job in a gambling casino if you want one? These and many other questions are on the minds of all Las Vegas visitors.

The wages in a casino vary, but the following are fairly typical. Lowest paid on the staff is "the shill," who for $10 a day, plays with the house money at a vacant table and tries to drum up trade, and leaves as soon as other players enter the game. A "change girl" circulating up and down the slot machine aisles can earn as much as $17 a day. The change girl in each booth in the casino takes home with her about $20. A dealer (whether at Blackjack, Roulette, or on any of the three "bases" of a Craps table—with a twenty-minute work-and-rest schedule) starts at $22.50 and can make as much as $25, plus *tips*. The "box man" or supervisor of each unit earns $40 and cannot accept gratuities. The "pit boss" and "shift boss" earn between $40 and $50 a day. The casino cashier, who handles the daily "bankroll" of over $800,000 a day, only puts $25 of it into her purse. As you can see casino salaries are not particularly high, and tips are in order the same as for any other service well performed. Tips are given to the stickman on the Craps table and are placed in his shirt pocket. The table personnel operate on a "pool" basis and all tips are added to the pool, and then divided equally. Incidentally, the drinks in a casino are free, but it is customary to tip the cocktail waitress.

Most of the Las Vegas casinos are fully staffed with permanent employees. It is obviously to their advantage to hire persons who have worked for them before or are known to the management, so employment is on the basis of individual selection by the casino. Most dealers serve two or three years in Casino Center before going to the Strip.

Private schools for the training of dealers exist. The dealers' school in Las Vegas concentrates on teaching the fundamental rules and practices of the game. It teaches what the dealer should do with his left hand and what he should do with his right hand and in what sequence, and what the dealer has to say while he is going through these manual actions. Graduation from a dealers' school is no automatic guarantee of a job, any more than a high school diploma or a college degree is. Dealers have to find jobs after first getting the training for it. In addition, some casinos prefer to train their own dealers.

There is *no* question about the honesty of the employees. Most of the *mythical* incidents of cheating are imaginative webs spun by frustrated suckers and habitual "gambleholics," who dumbly grope for excuses for their own failure to win. A casino cannot afford a dishonest employee. If one is caught at work in its establishment, the casino can lose its license. For this reason alone, there is far more regimentation by casino owners for the protection of their customers than can be found in other business.

The conditions under which casino employees are permitted to handle money are as strict as for those who work in the United States Mint. The mirrors on the walls or ceilings in most of the casinos, for instance, are not ordinary ones. They are specially made so that someone behind the reflecting surface can look through them as if they were ordinary window glass. Casinos are also protected by closed-circuit television in which a monitor can view all of the gambling games, the cashiers' cages, and the entrances and exits to the establishment. Uniformed guards and plain-clothes detectives are at work throughout the casino.

Female personnel are not allowed to carry their purses with them or wear clothes with large pockets. If an employee must put a hand in his or her pocket for any reason, it must be done in the following prescribed manner: the hands are exhibited, fingers outstretched with the palms upward, to show that nothing is concealed in them. Even when a handkerchief is withdrawn from a pocket it has to be dangled by one corner to show that nothing is being removed or replaced other than the handkerchief. There are other checks on an employee's honesty which we are not at liberty to describe here because such measures must be kept secret in order to be effective. All casino employees are fingerprinted and receive a routine Police Department checkup which they must pass before being hired. Remember that while your own risk as to an employee's honesty is only a small one, the casino's is a lot larger and you may rest assured that if the casino management was satisfied with an employee's record and references, and hired him, he is considered above reproach.

Sure, dealers can make errors, and on occasions they do. For this reason it is always wise to check the payoff. If the dealer makes an error, leave the bet and the payoff on the table and ask the dealer to check it. Should you still have a question, do not be afraid to ask him to clear up your problem for you. In the *very* infrequent cases that the dispute is not settled to your satisfaction at the table, ask to see the casino manager. If you still feel that you have been cheated, you can write to the Nevada State Gaming Control Board, Carson City, Nevada 89701.

It would be most foolish to say that Las Vegas is completely lily white. This would not be true, but when compared with other cities of the United States—and the world—the Fun Capital's record is remarkable. But, now that you've learned a little about Las Vegas' gambling, let us see how to survive (and perhaps prosper) at America's largest and favorite pastime.

2

♠

How to Survive
(and Perhaps Prosper)

Just after Desert Inn opened in 1950, a sailor (his name is still unknown) at a craps table made twenty-seven passes in a row, which means that he won twenty-seven times in a row. The sailor, a timid man, walked off winning $750. If he had left his original bet on the table, instead of pulling money out after each win, he would have won, if he had been fantastically lucky enough to quit at precisely the twenty-seventh pass, $268,435,456. As it was, this freakish achievement (the odds on twenty-seven passes in a row are 12,467,890 to 1) nonetheless cost the Desert Inn $150,000 from the side bets that were made by bettors at the table. Zeppo Marx, of the original Marx Brothers, won $30,000, and one patron who could not get near enough to the table to make a bet, offered $500 for a grandstand position. Nobody took him up. The sailor disappeared into the desert, but the dice he used repose to this day on a velvet pillow in a showcase in the Desert Inn's lobby, a kind of Las Vegas Crown Jewel.

This incident does not prove very much perhaps, but it does prove that despite the alarming stories in your Sunday newspapers, often written by people who have never thrown a pair of dice in their lives, you *can* win at Craps or at Roulette or at Blackjack or even at the slot machines. Organized gambling is based upon strict mathematical probabilities. The house does not always win—witness the case of the sailor—but in the long run it wins inexorably. The house is *reasonably* secure behind its odds. In the long haul,

15

they know that they are going to end up with a fair percentage of the money that crosses the table. They would just as soon you did not risk a pile on those long odds, because they have a nasty habit of paying off every now and then.

Everybody who gambles wants to win. According to Sam Landy, Las Vegas' famed Professor of Chance, 95 per cent of those who try it at the "Entertainment Capital of the World" would be ecstatic if they could make enough to pick up the tab for their meals, food and drinks, and maybe have a couple of silver dollars jingling in their pockets on the way home. After all, they had a ball, and it did not cost a nickel. They are the ones who play it cautious. They are thinking of the bills, and when the risk gets too great, they draw down. It is better to be safe than sorry.

What about the other 5 per cent? They are the ones, Sam says, who come to Las Vegas to win "important money." These are the characters who give the pit bosses the shivers. They know the odds, too, but they do not play with them; they bet against them. When the weak sisters are pulling their money back, these guys are pouring it on. When they win, it is damaging.

Do you have to be a millionaire to bet this way? No, says Sam. You can start with any amount: a dollar, five dollars, a hundred, or even a dime. It is a good idea to have a little bankroll to carry you over the rough spots, but with a fair amount of luck at the first, you do not need it.

There was a doctor from Des Moines who proved just that a few months back. He had been cleaned to the tune of $40 in one of the local card rooms. That was the total amount he had allocated himself for gambling, and, as it was gone, he excused himself from the table and started to leave the casino. He had exactly 25 cents left in his pockets. The doctor was running his fingers over his last quarter as he walked by the slot machines near the door, when the thought occurred to him, "If I'm going to be wiped out, I might as well do a thorough job of it."

He put the quarter in a machine, pulled the handle and watched disinterestedly as the three wheels sprang into action. Thunk . . . thunk . . . thunk . . . JACKPOT! Thirty-five dollars worth of quarters spewed down the chute. The good doctor realized he had to make a decision. He could take the $35 and leave. This would pull him all but $5 out of the hole. On the other hand . . . He had a hunch! He took his money to the roulette table and started playing, $5 at a time. When he hit, he let it ride. In a matter of minutes, he had $1,500. He moved to the craps table, where the action is faster, and started pushing the money out again. Two and one-half hours later the doctor from Des Moines left the casino. Only this time his mood was different. He had won $27,500, and he kept it!

The secret is, the doctor was willing to gamble. He could have taken his slot machine winnings and gone home only $5 light, but he took a chance and it paid off. This kind of thinking is not so preposterous as it might seem. For example, you go to the races and you bet the favorite every time for the first seven events, and every time he runs out of the money. Now comes the eighth and last race. Do you bet the favorite again, or do you put your money on the long shot? Certainly, the risk is far greater on the long shot, but if it comes in you are home free.

Now, do not construe this to mean you should always bet your cash on the long shot. Everyone has either experienced or heard of "lucky streaks" when those one-in-a-million chance numbers come up several times in succession. If you happen to be there and have your money down in the right place, you can make a fortune. But those formidable odds are against you. It might be just your luck that when you have your chips on the long shot, it will not come in at all. That might be the time when those dice, or the cards or the ball on the roulette wheel are making up for their previous "oversights," so as not to make a liar of the theory of probabilities.

Those odds that work against your having a winning streak have their effect upon the house, too. In fact, a greater effect, because you are a short-term gambler and therefore much more susceptible to "streaks," while the house, with its much greater volume of activity, feels the full weight of the law of probability. Theoretically, the house should win just as many bets as it loses, and nobody is going to invest in any kind of business on that basis, whether it be in a gambling casino, a drug store or a steel mill.

How do the gambling houses insure a return on their mountainous expenses? Not by cheating, because the risk of getting caught by Nevada's vigilant gambling control agencies and losing everything is much too great. And besides, it is highly unnecessary. How then?

Know the Odds and Probabilities

A casino makes its money because in most of its games skill cannot be of any real help to you. All the games except the card ones, are based upon chance, and regardless of what bet you may make, the casino pays off at less than true mathematical odds. You might say this is the "commission" the casino gets for running the game, taking the risk and providing all those other attractions that bring fifteen million visitors to Las Vegas each year. John Scarne, in his book, *Complete Guide to Gambling*, points out very succinctly how this operates.

Suppose, Scarne says, that you walk up to a carnival wheel with $15 in your pocket. The wheel is numbered 1 to 15, and the operator pays off winners at 10 to 1 odds. Suppose that you bet the same number every time for fifteen spins of the wheel, and the wheel hews strictly to probability and stops on that number one time out of the fifteen spins.

You have bet fifteen and won ten. The $1 you bet on the winner was returned to you, so you have a return of $11 for your $15 investment. The operator of the wheel made $4 on the transaction, which is his charge for running the game. If he had paid you at the true mathematical odds of 14 to 1, you would have broken even . . . and so would he. "This," Scarne says, "is what makes gambling operators rich and most players poor."

From this comes the amazing revelation that it is the winners who pay for the privilege of gambling, not the losers. When you lose your money at the table, it remains there and may be called upon moments later to pay off a winner. The casino actually is just a middleman for this kind of money. But when you win, the house chops off a percentage by paying you off at less than the mathematical odds. In doing so, the casino has made a profit on the transaction. This is exactly the same as "markup" in any other type of business, where a merchant buys his commodities wholesale and sells them retail. The difference in price pays all his expenses and overhead and, he hopes, gives him a reasonable profit.

This profit is known as house *percentage* or *advantage*. This percentage, or tax, is subtle, but it is always there. Let us say that you bet $1 on each toss of a coin—an even money proposition. But, instead of paying you $1 every time you win, the house pays only 99 cents, and when you lose it collects $1. That gives the house an advantage, or profit, of 1 per cent. While this seems like a minute amount, it could mean that if, at the end of a 1,000 tosses, you had won 500 and lost 500 of them, you would be out $5. It is possible, in the case of big house advantage bets, that even when a player has a lucky streak and wins, he ends up a loser. His chance to clean up has been greatly reduced because of high percentage.

The house percentages vary from game to game and bet to bet. Players who do not know what percentages they are up against do not realize that they are often paying much more for the privilege of gambling than they need to. The smart player avoids games and bets having high percentages against him. The table below indicates the range of house percentage in the more popular casino games:

Craps	0.83 to 16.7%
Blackjack or Twenty-One (expert play)	Under 1%
(average play)	2 to 3%
(poor play)	6% and up
Roulette	5.27 to 7.9%
Slot Machines	10 to 50%
Keno	20% and up
Bingo	Over 20%
Money Wheel	11.1 to 25.9%
Chuck-a-Luck	7.9 to 22.2%
Baccarat	1.06 to 1.23%
Faro	1.57%

The betting limits—both minimum and maximum—vary from casino to casino and game to game. For example, in Casino Center the minimum bet at Craps is 10 cents, at others 25 cents, while at all Strip casinos the minimum is $1. The exceptions to the $1 minimum bet at Strip games are slot machine play, with 5 cent, 10 cent, 25 cent, 50 cent, and $1 machines; Roulette, which has a 25 cent bet on the numbers; and Baccarat which has a minimum of $5 to $20. The Strip hotels have a maximum of $2,000 at Baccarat, $1,000 at Craps, and $500 at Twenty-One. At Craps, the maximum flat bet is $500 when odds of $500 are taken as well. At Blackjack, the maximum bet can be made again on split hands, and another $500 can be made on a double down play. There is, however, no maximum or minimum limits on your play, except if the table is closed for any reason. Slot machine play, Craps, Blackjack and Roulette are open on a twenty-four-hour basis. You can gamble for as long as your money holds out. Also there are no limits on the amount of money you can win, except the capital available to the casino. No player has ever "broken the bank at Las Vegas." In Nevada, unlike Monte Carlo, each table does not close down if it is "broken." Here, to "break the bank," one would have to break the entire house. And the odds against that are nearly impossible.

Speaking of odds, many players, including inveterate gamblers, confuse them with "chance," thinking that they are one and the same thing. But they are not. Chance is the possibility or probability of winning a bet you make, while odds give the difference or ratio between the chances of winning and not. In other words, it is the probability of failure in a given risk compared to the probability of success. The first figure given in an odds ratio is always the one for the probability of failure. A success probability of one chance in ten is the same as odds of 9 to 1. Actually, odds are given in order to equalize a wager that would otherwise be unfair.

In stating the odds of certain games, especially Craps, you must watch for the words "to" and "for." This psychological trick of some casino managements can cost you money if you are not careful. For instance, the meaning of the odds of 15 *to* 1 is that the winning payoff is fifteen betting units plus your initial bet—a total of sixteen units. Odds of 15 *for* 1 indicates that the winning payoff is fifteen units including your initial wager. In other words, you are receiving odds of 14 *to* 1.

In most of the casino games, the player *takes* the odds. That is, in a 2 to 1 situation, for instance, he takes the two units if he wins or pays one if he loses. In other words, the majority of the time he is on the "long end" of the odds. There are a few times, in Craps, for example, when it is possible for the player to lay the odds. In this instance, he is on the "short end" of the odds, say 5 to 11, which means that if he wins he receives five units from the house or when losing, gives up eleven.

ODDS TO PERCENTAGE PROBABILITY

Odds	Percentage Probability	Odds	Percentage Probability	Odds	Percentage Probability
Shorter than 1–100	Quasi-certitude	1–2	66.667	9–2	18.182
		8–15	65.217	5–1	16.667
		4–7	63.656	11–2	15.385
		8–13	61.905	6–1	14.286
		4–6	60.000	13–2	13.333
1–100	99.010	8–11	57.895	7–1	12.500
1–50	98.039	4–5	55.556	15–2	11.765
1–33	97.059	6–5	54.545	8–1	11.111
1–25	96.154	10–11	52.381	9–1	10.000
1–20	95.238	20–21	51.220	10–1	9.091
8–100	92.593	Evens	50.000	100–9	8.257
1–10	90.909	21–20	48.780	100–8	7.407
1–9	90.000	11–10	47.619	100–7	6.542
1–8	88.889	5–6	45.455	100–6	5.660
2–15	88.236	5–4	44.444	18–1	5.263
1–7	87.500	11–8	42.105	20–1	4.762
2–13	86.667	6–4	40.000	22–1	4.348
1–6	85.714	13–8	38.095	25–1	3.846
2–11	84.615	7–4	36.364	33–1	2.941
1–5	83.333	15–8	34.783	40–1	2.439
2–9	81.818	2–1	33.333	50–1	1.961
1–4	80.000	9–4	30.769	66–1	1.493
2–7	77.778	5–2	28.571	100–1	0.990
30–100	76.923	11–4	26.667		
1–3	75.000	3–1	25.000		
4–11	73.333	100–30	23.077		
2–5	71.429	7–2	22.222	Greater than 100–1	Insignificant chances
4–9	69.231	4–1	20.000		

Almost every scientific study of gambling starts with an analysis of what occurs when a coin is spun, and we shall do the same. Unless bias is in any way present, the chance that the result will be *heads* will nearly be equal to the chance that it will be *tails*. But, every spin is independent of another, and there is no more likelihood of a *head* turning up following a *tail* than there is of another *tail*. Even if *tails* turns up twenty times in succession it will not be in the slightest astonishing for the sequence to remain unbroken with the twenty-first spin. True, many players think that a *head* is more likely to turn up than *tails* because they believe that "law of averages" states that *heads* and *tails* must eventually come up an equal number of times. Let us emphasize one very important fact: the theory of probability, or law of averages, is just a mathematical prediction of what may be expected to happen in the long run, not a law that says that certain things must inevitably happen. Thus when you toss a coin, the theory of probability says that *heads* will turn up approximately half the time in the long run. It does not say that in a very long run *heads* and *tails* must come up exactly the same number of times.

Statistical coin-spinning experiments have indicated that the difference between actual and expected results often increases over long runs. For instance, in a series of one hundred spins, the results may be forty-five or fifty-five *heads* rather than the expected fifty. If the number of tosses were increased to 10,000, the deviation between actual and expected results may have increased to fifty under or over the predicted 5,000. In the first case, the percentage of deviation was 10 per cent (5/50), while in the second, the difference percentage was only 1 per cent (50/5000). As you can see, the percentage of deviation between the actual and expected results does tend to decrease in the long run. But it is only in this sense that the results seem to "even up."

Failure to understand the theory of probability costs many players a chance to win "big" money. Let us see how this affects the casino and the individual player. Since the casino makes so many more bets than any one player in a single gambling session, the house experiences a much longer run and thus its wins and losses will usually conform rather closely to what the theory of probability says it can expect. On the other hand, the individual player, even in an extended series of gaming sessions, could be considered only a short run. His winning and losing, therefore, may vary a great deal from his long-run expectation. This is the fact that many players fail to realize. That is, when they are on a "hot," or winning, streak, they are afraid to ride with it because they believe the chances of a "cold," or losing, streak setting in are constantly increasing. Likewise, when losing steadily, they insist on continuing because they think the "law" states that the longer they lose the more certain they can be that their fortunes are bound to change. Remember that a game of chance is just that, a game of chance. If there were any sure knowledge, it would not be "chancy." As long as every roll, spin or card has many possibilities, who is to know for sure what is going to happen?

It is important, however, to keep in mind that there are definite ways to increase your chances of winning. And you *can* win at Las Vegas. But how can this be possible when:

1. *The house has a mathematical advantage on every bet you place.* This is very true because as you will see in the following chapters the house never pays off at true odds.

2. *Because of this mathematical advantage, the house stands to win from a half-cent to over 20 cents on every dollar you bet.* Again, this is a correct statement since the house's percentage is a tax taken out from the money wagered.

3. *Theoretically you lose this amount every time you place a bet.* Another statement that is true because of the house's built-in advantage. But even though you are betting constantly with the percentages against you, it is possible to beat the house during your stay in Las Vegas by judicious play, good money management, a little luck—and the theory of probability.

If you stay at the gambling table for an extended period of time, you will in all probability lose. Gambling casino operation is based, as stated previously, on the theory of probability too, and the fact that if millions of dollars of wagers are made the house will make a profit which is in direct ratio to the percentages it has in its favor. For instance, if $20,000,000 is bet over a period of a year and the overall house's percentage is 1½ per cent, the casino is *pretty certain* of netting a profit of $300,000. You note that we said pretty certain. Because nothing is mathematically improbable, a house pitted against unlimited capital over an indefinite period of time *could* run into a series of losses that would break it. Several of Las Vegas casinos have gone bankrupt.

Remembering that all things are possible, here is a supposition that is worth thinking about. If a thousand "expert" gamblers took about $25,000 and interminably made wagers against Las Vegas casinos, several of the gamblers would go broke within a few weeks. A couple would go on as long as they lived. A few would last six months or so, a few would last only a year. The majority, according to computer tests, would last for five to ten years and from time to time would be ahead of the game until that inevitable last time when the house advantage would break them. Actually, the two things that knock an expert player off eventually are the house's percentage and prolonged losing streaks. Obviously it behooves the player to select a game in which the house advantage is least against him and manage his money properly until Lady Luck comes along.

Luck and Hunches

Understanding luck is an integral part of gambling. Unfortunately, it is a very intangible thing. One modern-day dictionary defines it as "that which happens to one seemingly by chance." In an ancient Roman dictionary it might have been termed "the result of the gods." But, whatever definition you use, it plays a most important part in gambling. Actually, many of the casino games—Craps, Keno, Slot Machines, Roulette, Chuck-a-Luck, Wheel of Fortune, Baccarat, Faro—are based on just pure luck. Even Blackjack, Pan and Poker in a casino are games of luck, but since you are given some choice in your play, your skill will have an effect upon the amount that you win or lose.

Luck seems to run in cycles. There are times when nothing goes right and times when everything is favorable. Thus, many times gambling is a "matter of proper timing." It is "good luck" when you are on a winning streak; "bad luck" when experiencing a losing cycle. It is the element of the unknown—whether a cycle, good or bad, is beginning or in the process of ending—that adds extra excitement to the sport of gambling.

Human emotions such as hunches and superstitions play a major role in gambling, too. When in a game of Craps, for instance, a shooter picks up the dice, all the other players throw immediate glances in his direction, and if they like his looks, or if the shooter wears something attractive, or they like him for any one of a hundred different reasons—reasons which, in the end, prove to be just plain hunches—they will bet accordingly. You would be surprised at the reasons players give for betting certain ways.

During my many stays in Las Vegas, I have met several players who actually felt a sort of personal relationship with the dice. After a long losing streak, they would demand new cubes, complaining that the old ones had it in for them and were losing on purpose. It is very important to know that the two dice cannot *see, hear or smell.* Dice cannot remember who shot them last or what number was thrown last. Nor do they know what number will come up in the next throw, for that action is in the hands of Lady Luck. But players often imagine certain things that the dice can and will do because of certain emotions or happenings around the table. If the dice hit a player's hand, for instance, the shooter will blame him for a 7 showing up, for according to the shooter, a 7 will always come up when the dice hit a player's hand. (Well, almost always.) Or if a player is really doing well, and should his wife join him at *this moment,* he is bound to lose on the next roll, because wives have been known to be "death" to a husband.

Do not laugh at all this. You will probably pick up a superstition or two during your gambling days. *All* gamblers believe in luck despite the fact that we know that mathematics, probability and the odds are all with the house. This belief in luck and a universal wish to control it—or at least keep it—is what is at the root of most popular gambling superstitions. For instance, my wife, when she plays a slot machine, raises her left foot, because in the past she has hit several jackpots in this manner. Asinine, of course, but I do have my lucky sports jacket which I *must* wear while I gamble in Las Vegas casinos.

Does superstition have any influence on gambling? Yes and unfortunately it is usually to the depredation of the player. That is, he will often defeat himself once he gives full sway to a superstition. And once a gambler loses complete control of a situation and has allowed anything other than *good* play techniques to influence his judgment, he is bound to lose.

If your superstitions do not affect the logic of play, by all means keep them. They are a part of gambling. Sam Landy, who has an excellent collection of stories of gamblers' hunches and superstitions, tells about a woman who followed every move made by a drunk at a gaming table. Every time the inebriated one placed a bet, she would put her own right alongside. This went on for several plays, and finally a companion asked the woman: "Why do you watch that drunk and make every bet he does?"

"Because," the lady answered, "they tell me the Good Lord takes care of fools and drunks, so I'm with him!"

It might be unfair to the "science" of parapsychology to include the subjects of extra-sensory perception (ESP) and psychokinesis (PK) in the section on superstition and luck. In recent years a great deal has been written on what influence these subjects will have on the gambling industry. While believers in ESP and PK make great claims, casino owners have not yet noted any decrease in profits because of parapsychology. If you believe in ESP and PK, that is fine, but do not let it interfere with good play practices.

Every player has hunches, and so do the casino bosses. If you think that you are immune to them, then either you have an extremely analytical mind, or you have never been carried away by the super-fast action and nerve-wracking excitement of casino games. While it may be good, on rare occasions, to play your hunches, do *not* let them control your play. Gamble with a clear mind, a mind uncluttered with your emotional feeling, intuitions and superstititions. And while there is a certain amount of luck involved in all gambling, never substitute it for your knowing the game—the rules, the betting, and the percentages. You will find that you will win more often.

Good Money Management

If you expect to win *big* when Lady Luck is on your side, you must know how to manage your money correctly. "There is no question about it, proper management of your money is the most important part of gambling," according to Las Vegan Rod Morris. Rod presumably knows, since he not only is a veteran dealer himself, but an operator of the Nevada School of Dealing, which trains the employees of many of the casinos.

Before starting any gambling venture in Las Vegas, as previously stated, set an *absolute* limit that you are willing to lose. This sounds like a rather easy rule to follow, but the cashiers' windows at the casinos are usually plagued by players who wish credit beyond the limits they themselves set. Remember that this limit was established on the basis of your sound judgment under rational circumstances, and any attempt to increase this amount upon the depletion of your betting funds during the rigors of play is an emotional reaction of poor judgment. Never embarrass yourself, or the credit manager, by asking for a further extension of credit once you have reached the limit you set for your losses.

Incidentally, this limit should be an amount that you will not miss if you lose, or an amount that you would consider as spent on entertainment. That is, never bet the mortgage payment on the house or money for the baby's shoes. In order to become a "smart" player, you must have a worry-free mind. And you cannot have a clear chain of thought if you are playing with money you are afraid of losing. Therefore, be sure that you can afford your losses *before* you lose.

It is a good idea to divide your budgeted gambling capital between the various planned gaming sessions prior to your arrival in Vegas. In other words, set aside so much money for each day's gambling session rather than possibly blowing your entire limit quickly and spoiling your entire trip. Many people divide their daily sessions into four one-to-two-hour segments: morning, pre-dinner show, in between shows, and post-midnight show. This leaves the afternoon free for golf, swimming, and the many other outdoor activities available. But remember that it takes a degree of discipline to follow a predetermined limit for the entire gambling trip, for each individual day, and for each proposed gaming session. Failure to follow any part of your gaming capital plan will effectively circumvent your entire plan and can result in a frustrating time. While Las Vegas is the fun capital of the world, it can be a most exasperating place without gambling stakes.

All casino games except slot machines and Baccarat use chips rather than cash. Your money can be changed into chips directly at the playing table, but there is no provision for any change in cash and you will receive chips for the entire amount. Personal checks and travelers checks, on approval of the credit manager, will be cashed by the casino cashier in either cash or chips, or any desired combination. For all chip denominations of $5 or more, the chips are legal tender in Las Vegas. They will be accepted without question at any other casino, store, or even as a contribution at the church of your faith. The metal tokens, however, are limited in use to the issuing casino. All chips and tokens can be cashed in at the casino cashier's cage. The exception to this is the colored chips used at the Roulette layouts which are handled exclusively at the table where they are issued. More on Roulette and its special chips can be found in Chapter 5.

At the start of any gaming session, keep your bets small until you test your luck. If that nebulous female we call "Lady Luck" is on your side, increase your bets accordingly. On the other hand, if you lose six or eight bets in a row, stop for a couple of rounds, change tables, or go for a walk. Always press your luck when winning; never when you are losing.

Failure to follow this simple rule is why the casinos can afford such lavish furnishings and offer such fabulous entertainment. Most visitors to Las Vegas follow this rule in reverse. The average tourist generally has a fixed gaming trip and session limit in mind and does keep his first few bets small. But, after losing three or four bets in a row, he begins to have an uneasy feeling. After all, he plans to spend a week in Las Vegas and must start winning some big money soon. So he gets an inspirational hot flash and doubles his bet because the "law of averages" says that he is certain to win. The result of the next round is the same—he loses. Thus, he triples his bets in order to recoup all his losses with a win. After a few bets like this his gaming session limits are reached. He does not, however, stop; he continues to increase bets until all his Las Vegas trip capital is gone. Thus, in possibly less than an hour's time, he has ruined his planned week's stay in Las Vegas. This is a true story; it happens hundreds of times a day. Do not let it happen to you.

It is wise at the beginning to keep your single bets from 3 to 5 per cent of your total gaming session capital until you start winning and are playing with house money. By betting this percentage of your capital until you begin to win, you will not be wiped out before you have had a run for your money, and it is large enough so that you have an opportunity to win big. In other words, this arrangement provides you the opportunity to weather unfavorable runs of reasonable length, while still providing sufficient money to capitalize on a favorable streak should one occur.

Your dilemma is, of course, that no one can predict when a good run will begin; and, once a good streak has begun, it is impossible to say when it will end. But, as soon as you go ahead of the house, begin to increase the size of your bets. Thus, your object is always to get to the position where you are able to make big sum bets. To make such bets with your own money could be disastrous. But when using house money it is a different thing, so bet big.

Sam Landy tells a story that is most apropos: "Several years ago, a friend of mine went to the crap table and started with $500. In a few minutes, he was down to $40, and although he was a wealthy man, he was disturbed. The dice came around to him, and I asked to shoot the dice for him, so he gave me the 40 bucks. In those days, the house limit was $200. Well, I held the dice for one hour and five minutes. After the hand was over, I had won over $10,400 and had $2,600 on the table when I lost the hand. I won that money not because I am any *luckier* than him, but because I had the *guts, especially with someone else's dough!*"

The moral of Sam's story is simple: When playing with house money (*someone else's dough*), bet with plenty of nerve (*guts*). It is almost impossible to win "big" money if you stay at the same level bet after bet. Suppose, for example, you won ten bets in a row. Ten bets in a row at $1 each would be, at even odds, $10 winnings. But if you let the money ride until you reach the limit of the house (generally $500), you could win $1,012.

While letting the winnings ride on the table, or parlaying it, until the house's limit is reached is the quickest way to win big money, most smart players prefer the "safer" slow progression system. This should not be misconstrued as a *betting system* (see page 34). It is a method to get you into a progressive betting pattern during favorable runs, and allows you to bet accordingly. It is interesting to note that when big winning streaks do occur, they take place for a player over a period of time *usually* not exceeding twenty minutes. The remainder of the average gaming session normally shows a loss, or a small profit at best. The laws of probability do not call for unusual favorable runs to occur often, so be sure to capitalize on them when such situations do arise. Never walk away from a winning streak.

To see how the slow progression system operates, let us suppose you are a $2 bettor. Your original bet is $2. If you lose, continue your $2 bet. If you win a hand, bet $4. If you win again, bet $6. If you win the next bet, wager $10. If you win the $10 bet, stay at the same amount for the next. If you win again, jump your next bet to $15 and stay at this limit until you lose a bet. Then revert back to your $2 bet. Always revert to your original wager after each bet you lose. For instance, if you lose on the second bet, which was $4, return to your $2 wager on the next one.

In this manner, you become a $15 bettor when winning and a $2 bettor when losing. You are more relaxed playing this way than betting $15 when losing and $2 when winning. Most small bettors feel uncomfortable when making high wagers. The average $2 player is generally most happy and grateful to win a few hundred dollars now and then. This is a good take for the average Las Vegas tourist and can be done if the money is bet and managed properly. Incidentally, only about 1 per cent of the players that gamble in Las Vegas ever reach or bet the $500 limit.

The following is a table showing the progression of consecutive *winning* bets for players at various established bets:

If You Are Betting	Slow Progression of Winning Bets
$1	$1, $2, $3, $5, $5, $8, $10 *
$2	$2, $4, $6, $10, $10, $15 *
$5	$5, $10, $15, $25, $25, $35, $50 *
$10	$10, $20, $30, $50, $50, $75, $100 *
$25	$25, $50, $75, $125, $125, $150, $200 *
$50	$50, $100, $150, $225, $225, $300 *
$100	$100, $200, $300, $400, $400, $500

* Stay at this limit until you lose a bet. Then revert to your original bet.

By playing a slow progression, you will notice that after winning two hands in a row your profit takes care of the third bet. The next winning hands in succession are all free hands and you are not supplying the money. You will also note that the fourth and fifth bets are the same amount. This is a sort of cushion if you win both of these bets. Should you lose the next wager, you will be in a comfortable position when you start with your original bet again. Some players call this their "playing money," while others "lock-it-up." In other words, the latter players take the locked up money out of the game; not to be gambled again. Really, this money is the player's profit. It can only be considered a profit, however, when the money *leaves* Las Vegas. How many times have you heard of the big wins that are ultimately lost back to the casinos? Therefore, when you decide to lock up a portion of winnings—a smart player always does—make certain that money gets home. A check mailed there with the proceeds of your winnings removes any temptation to give it back to the casino and is a wonderful souvenir which could help bring you back to Las Vegas on your next vacation trip.

While it is a good idea to take your profit out of the game, never "drag down" as long as you are winning when employing the slow progressive system. Therefore, do not try to guess when you are going to lose. You cannot. If you start guessing, it will be your downfall. Remember that every round is a new hand. Forget the previous play—win, lose or draw. If you have made a mistake, forget about it. There is nothing you can do to rectify it now. Do not let it interfere with playing the next round or hand.

In playing a slow progression system, should your hand in Blackjack, for example, call for doubling down or splitting pairs, do not hesitate one bit regardless of what amount you are betting; you must play the hand, not the money. That is, proper play should never be affected by the size of the wager. When you have a large bet staring you in the face, just remember how you accomplished this—only one way: by playing and managing your money properly. You may lose some bets, but win others. When betting house money be brave, when betting your own be a coward. This is the key to winning important money at a casino. In other words, increase your bets during a favorable run, and avoid increasing bets during an unfavorable streak.

A smart player, as stated earlier, follows one adage religiously, and that is to make sure he is always getting the best possible odds. Select a game which offers you close to a 50 per cent chance of winning. Information on the odds and how to use them to the player's best advantage are fully discussed in the remaining chapters of this book. Be sure to follow the advice given, because good play goes hand in hand with proper money management. Also, it is easy to let the many casino distractions interfere with playing concentration, which can affect the control of your money, too.

The player who has trained to use the methods described in the following chapters *must* be able to keep his attention on the game. Casino owners will tell you, with complete candor, that their establishments are designed to inhibit your judgment and to subtly encourage an emotional approach to gambling. For many first-timers, the initial impact of the casino atmosphere is too much for them to cope with. Thus, it is most important to follow the suggestion given on page 11 to the letter. Actually, it is a good idea before beginning any gaming session to walk about the casino, observe game play, make some *mental* bet and study player reactions. But, once you are fully acclimated to the casino environment and decide to begin your gambling session, give your complete and undivided attention to your game. If you cannot do this, then do not play at that time.

During play, avoid social talk with your fellow players. Do not annoy the dealers with small talk. Most of them do an excellent job of patiently putting up with the gripes and barbs of idiots, who try to camouflage their losses and incompetence with their big mouths. If you cannot concentrate at one table because of other players' idiosyncrasies or distractions, relax a few minutes and try a new table. It is generally wise to limit your gaming session to an hour or two. Serious gambling is a tiring sport, and fatigue can cause costly errors. If you feel tired, stop play. Put your money away and come back when you feel well rested and mentally alert. Remember that action is available in Las Vegas twenty-four hours a day.

It is wise to vary your play to include more than one type of casino game. One of the reasons that Baccarat has become such a popular game is that it offers a fine break and relaxation after playing Craps and Twenty-One.

Do not drink excessively while gambling because your judgment is seriously impaired. Your senses are dulled and you are unable to calculate wisely or swiftly. Therefore, save your drinking for afterwards, either for celebrating a win or consoling a loss.

Sex is another distraction that should be avoided during gambling. By reading certain exposé books on Las Vegas, you may be of the belief that illicit sex is rampant there. While it may shatter some illusions, nothing is further from the truth. The casinos are on a constant vigil to keep hustlers out of their gaming areas. The reason for this is most understandable. Since the casino is in the business of gambling, their profits are maximum when they can keep a player active at the gaming tables. Any diversion from this activity reduces profits, and, employing good business sense, the casinos attempt to cut down the sex distractions as much as possible. Since it cannot be completely eliminated, always be sure to keep your mind on the game when gambling. It would be most naïve to say that sex is not available in Las Vegas . . . as it is in most cities. And there have even been reports that big winners have sometimes been enticed to stay in town for further gambling sessions by a charming companion supplied by the casino management. Since the theory of probability and the house advantage are at their best for the casino over an extended period, this is just good business practice. Without discussing the moral issue, such a practice is, however, a poor bet for the player as far as money management is concerned.

Before leaving the subject of money management, there is one more point. Do not be a "happy loser." In all Las Vegas casinos, you can find a player who spends $50 in slot machines, then suddenly hits a $10 jackpot. After a free drink on the house, he puts $10 right back into the same winning machine. As he leaves the premises, he remarks with a big smile, "Oh, well, I didn't expect to win anyway. Just came down to pass some time away, and I figured I'd spend about $50."

You would be surprised how many people make that or similar remarks, and not only around the slots, but also at the Blackjack table or the Roulette wheel or Craps table. So, to all the people who come to Las Vegas with the avowed purpose of losing $50 or $100 we will say, on behalf of the casino owners in the city, "Welcome, sucker. Come again, and come often—as often as you can." There is an old expression around the casinos that goes like this: "Show me a happy loser, and I'll show you an idiot!"

Betting Systems

On paper betting systems offer intriguing reading, but they cannot possibly improve your chance of winning at Las Vegas' casinos. The fallacy with most of them is that they are based on misconceptions of the theory of probability and failure to consider the house's favorable advantage. This percentage is always there and enables the casino to pay its expenses and make a profit for its owners. As has already been stated, it is an indisputable fact that if you play at any casino game long enough the house advantage will surely catch up with you.

In Craps, for example, a 1.41 per cent house advantage means that each time $100 worth of bets is won by the players on the line bets the house should have paid off $101.41—if the exact odds were to be given. But they are not. If they were, the casinos could not operate. The odds, then—even if they are minute—are against the player. No matter how you may try to evade this incontrovertible fact, you cannot: When playing over a *long* period of time, you should expect to lose. This is true no matter what "infallible" betting system you are using.

Ever since the first bet was wagered, there have been betting systems. Some have become legendary classics due to the fact that, over the short haul, huge fortunes have been won while players were employing them. It is a moot question, however, whether these winnings were the results of the system or a player's temporary lucky streak. While we can assure you that it was because of the latter, here are a few of the more popular betting systems that have been adaptable to Craps, Blackjack and Roulette:

Martingale System. This is one of the oldest and most publicized systems. It is the double-or-nothing type of play that is common to almost all gambling and is extremely simple. After each *loss*, the previous bet is doubled; on a win, the system calls for a return to one betting unit.

There are two built-in flaws with the Martingale System. First, it is based on "the law of averages," which we know is no "law," since spin of the wheel or roll of the dice or toss of a card is an independent affair with no relationship to previous or future events. This, as you can see even at a house minimum of $1, amounts to a great deal of money.

Play	Stake	Total Loss
1st	$ 1	$ 1
2nd	$ 2	$ 3
3rd	$ 4	$ 7
4th	$ 8	$ 15
5th	$ 16	$ 31
6th	$ 32	$ 63
7th	$ 64	$ 127
8th	$128	$ 255
9th	$256	$ 511
10th	$512	$1,023

The second drawback with this system is house limit. That is, you cannot double your bet many times before reaching the maximum bet the house will accept—which is $500 in most Las Vegas casinos. As indicated above, after nine consecutive losses the system would fail because the casino would accept only $500 of the $512 bet necessary under the system. If that bet loses as well, where does the system player go from there?

Grand Martingale System. In this system, which is a sophisticated variation of the Martingale System, the player jumps an additional unit after each *loss*. For instance, when the first bet, $1, is lost the next bet is $3, winning back the dollar lost on the first bet and two others, one for each bet made. The third bet is $7, recouping the $4 lost with $3 additional, one for each bet. The complete Martingale is 1, 3, 7, 15, 31, 63, 127, 255, and 511, nine bets in all and the total loss $1,023 if all bets are lost. If the player wins the ninth bet he gathers in all his losses and $9 as a bonus. Actually, the ninth bet carries him $11 beyond the maximum. Runs of nine come with great frequency and the "Grand Martingale" gallops the foolish adherent to this system right over the edge of the cliff. It would take a lot of playing to win back $1,023 a dollar at a time, barring the risk of another run of nine.

Little Martingale System. This variation is used in any number of "short" systems. The player works from a stake of seven units, for example, betting one unit as the first bet, two as the second and four as the third, taking his *loss* of seven units and starting all over again at one unit.

In summary, the fault with all variations of the Martingale System (there are dozens of others that we did not mention) is that they provide very small gains while you are winning (all drop back to one unit bets when winning) and very large losses when you are losing. Over a long period of time you can expect to lose an amount equal to the total amount wagered multiplied by the house advantage of the bet made.

The D'Alembert System. In this system, which is very simple in its mathematics, you simply raise your bet $1 when you lose and lower it $1 when you win. If, for instance, your first bet is $5 and you win, your second bet should be $4. But if you lose then your second bet should be $6. The theory of this system is based on the law of averages, which *assumes*, as we have stated so many times, that you win and lose an equal number of times. *If* such circumstances did prevail, of course, you would emerge a winner with this system. But, since the law of averages cannot be trusted, neither can the system.

The Ascot System. The basis of this system is the following series of numbers which are known as the Ascot progression:

3, 6, 9, 12, 20, 25, 35, 50, 75, 125, 200

The player begins at 25 and bets upward in the series as long as he wins, downward as he loses. If he should win the 200 or lose the 3, he then begins all over again with his initial bet of 25 units.

The Labouchère System. This system, also known as the "cancellation system," is fairly complex and at the very least it should permit you to have a fairly long run before losing your money. It is based on increasing your bets while you lose the small ones and win the larger ones. Because of its complexity the beginner needs a pad and pencil in order to keep track of the betting.

The system is best explained by using the example of the series of 1–1, which provides a win of two units on completion. Here is how it works:

The bet is always the sum of the first and last numbers in the series, in this case: $1 + 1 = 2$. For a winning decision the objective

of winning two betting units has been accomplished and the series
is begun anew. In the case of a loss the amount of the losing bet is
added to the end of the series, and the series becomes 1–1–2. Again
the next bet is the sum of the first and last numbers in the series:
$1 + 2 = 3$. For a winning decision the first and last numbers are
crossed out, ̶1̶–1–2–̶2̶, and the next bet is the sum of the first and
last numbers in the series, $1 + 2 = 3$. If only one number remains
this would be the amount of the next bet. A subsequent win would
complete the series with an overall win of two units. If no numbers
remain, you start all over again with 1–1. The player's record sheet
is shown here for the case of Loss, Loss, Win, Win, Loss, Loss,
Win and Win sequence:

Series	Size of Bet	Loss	Win
1,1	$1 + 1$	2	
1,1,2	$1 + 2$	3	
1,1,2,3,	$1 + 3$	4	
1,1,2,3,4	$1 + 4$	5	
1,1,2,3,4,5	$1 + 5$		6
̶1̶,1,2,3,4,̶5̶	$1 + 4$		5
̶1̶,2,3,̶4̶	$2 + 3$	5	
2,3,5	$2 + 5$	7	
2,3,5,7	$2 + 7$		9
̶2̶,3,5,̶7̶	$3 + 5$		8
	Total Units	$\overline{26}$	$\overline{28}$

The results of the above example—six losing decisions to four
winning ones and yet a profit of two units—has led players to
believe that the Labouchère System overcomes the house percentage advantage. Unfortunately, this is not the case. True, a player
who is adequately financed will win during most of his gambling
session. During his few losing sessions, however, he will lose his
entire capital. And to be "successful" in the Labouchère System,
you must have a betting capital of at least 200 times the win
expectation of the series. Thus, for a series of 1–1, a betting capital
of 400 units is required.

Incidentally, the Labouchère System can be started with any
series of numbers: 1–2–3, 4–5–6, 8–9, etc. But in all cases, the
amount of the win is equal to the sum of the series when all
numbers are crossed out by wins. The larger the potential win,

however, the larger the capital needed to ride out a losing streak of reasonable duration. The capital requirement for an 8–9 series, for instance, would be a minimum of at least 3,400 betting units.

There are many other systems in use in Las Vegas. Some are pretty far out, incorporating the principles of Zen or any other theological philosophy which happens to be in current vogue. Players have even developed their own based on their astrological forecasts, lucky numbers, or their dreams of the previous night. But, regardless of the system, the house advantage will always prevail and it is doomed to failure.

Earlier, we discussed the slow progression system. At that time, it was stated that in reality it was *not* a betting system because it was not based on losing. That is, it was to be used *only* when a player is winning. There are other progression systems that may be employed, too. For instance, the so-called "*Anti*-Martingale System" requires doubling of the wager after a win for a pre-determined number of favorable runs. On completion of this sequence, the amount of the bet reverts to the start of the series, and the sequence is repeated. Let us say, for example, that the betting progression is 1, 2, 4, and 8. If you win the sequence of four, you go back to wagering one betting unit after the fourth win and start all over again. The Anti-Martingale System continues only for successive wins; a loss would terminate the series and it would begin anew with one betting unit in the same manner as the slow progression. Actually, any *reasonable* progression system that is in effect only while winning is generally acceptable. It is just good money management to play "big" with house money. Winning streaks seem to occur very seldom, so when one does arrive you must capitalize on its brief presence to overcome the house percentage.

Let us summarize the "seven-lucky" points that may help you to survive at the gambling tables of Las Vegas:

1. Exert a sincere effort to develop proficiency in the casino game or games you wish to enjoy. Full details of the play of all casino games are given in Chapters 3 to 9.

2. Set aside a gaming capital that you feel you can spend, or afford to lose, and keep within the limits of that sum. Then divide this gaming capital between the various planned gambling ses-

sions. Also limit your gambling session losses to the budgeted amount.

3. Know the exact betting odds and house percentages of the games in which you intend to indulge. Avoid all bets where you can lose far more than you stand to win, even if you should win.

4. Never make *single* bets more than 3 to 5 per cent of your total capital until you are playing with house money. Remember that no betting system works at games having a house advantage.

5. Manage your money properly. Use a progression system during favorable runs. "Lock-up" part of your winnings not to be gambled again.

6. Do not increase your bet during an unfavorable run. Always walk away from a losing streak. Leave a table if you lose six to eight bets in a row, and try another casino if two consecutive tables prove unlucky.

7. Limit your gaming sessions to two hours or less. If you feel fatigued, stop play. Also never drink to excess while gambling.

No one can, of course, tell you how to win at Las Vegas since no one knows—for sure. But the casino owners, dealers and pit bosses who furnished the information for the remaining chapters can tell you how to bet to win, taking advantage of what they know about house percentages and odds. They can explain the wagers you should avoid and what bets to make under various circumstances. In short, the rest of the book is devoted to taking most of the gamble out of gambling, but the little that is left is what makes life so exciting in Las Vegas. And it is this excitement that makes gambling such a popular "sport." It is this excitement that makes the shills, dealers, pit bosses, and even the casino owners gamble.

You ask yourself, "Is this possible? If anyone knows the odds, these people should. Why in the world would they turn right around and gamble themselves?" Sam Boyd, owner of the Eldorado Club in nearby Henderson, tells us the answer.

"They gamble at their own games because they know it is possible to win," he says. "There are a lot of losers at their tables, but there are some pretty big winners, too. They figure that with their superior knowledge of the game, and the odds, they can play much more intelligently."

Some of them do and some of them don't. If nothing more, they know better than most how to minimize their losses, but they are subject to the same human frailties as the next man. Sam Boyd tells a story about a dealer who used to work for him, by the name of Checkers. It was a few years ago when it was the practice to pay casino employees every day at the end of their shift. After taxes, Checkers got about $18, and he decided one day to see if he could increase his wages at the tables. It is a strict policy that dealers never gamble at their own clubs, so Checkers went across the street to another casino and started betting.

The next morning after Sam checked into his office he received a phone call from the owner of the other casino. "I doubt that your Checkers will be in for work this morning," he told Sam. "He was in my casino all night and won himself thirty thousand bucks."

"No kidding," replied Sam. "Did he keep it?"

"I'm happy to say he didn't," the other owner said. "The character got stinkin' drunk and blew every cent he had. I felt sorry for him, so I put two one dollar bills in his watch pocket and sent him home in a cab."

A short time later, Checkers did show up for work, though somewhat the worse for his ordeal the night before. He told Sam his tale of woe, that he had been cleaned out across the way, and asked for a draw to buy breakfast. "Are you sure you don't have any money?" Sam asked him.

"I've checked all my pockets. Not a dime!"

Sam insisted that he try his watch pocket, and watched Checkers' bloodshot eyes brighten as he produced the two folded bills. "By golly, Mr. Boyd," he exclaimed, "I didn't do so bad after all. You know, I only started with $18."

3

Craps—An Ancient Game Gets a New Shake

Egyptians, Babylonians, Greeks, and Romans of antiquity all enjoyed dice games. Craps is the favorite of serious gamblers because (1) it is a fast-moving game, and (2) it gives the shooter almost even-up odds for his money (244 to 251). In addition, the craps table layouts, such as those found in the Las Vegas casinos, give the player an infinite variety of exciting side bets in addition to the basic game.

Craps, of course, is played extensively anywhere that dice can be rolled on a flat surface. True, most people begin shooting Craps at private games for coins, or maybe bills, with their fellows. But, just in case you have never played the game at all or are a beginner, we will start with the fundamentals of play.

You throw a pair of dice, two perfectly square cubes, bearing dots 1 to 6 inclusive. Should the dots total 7 or 11 on the first roll, you win your bet, and the throw is called a "natural." If the dice add to 2, 3 or 12 on the first roll, it is "craps" and you lose. You keep the dice, however, and throw again.

When you as the shooter win, it is called a "pass." When you lose, it is called a "miss." This is not always, however, determined on the first roll. Instead of a "natural"—7 or 11—or a "craps"—2, 3 or 12—a 4, 5, 6, 8, 9 or 10 may appear. Then, any such number becomes your "point" and you try to "make the point" by rolling it again before a 7 appears. Here, 7 is no longer lucky. Also, 2, 3, 11 and 12 have no meaning when you are attempting to "make the point." You keep on shooting until you "pass" by bringing up the needed point or until you "miss" by rolling a 7. If you "pass," you win, keep the dice, and start a new sequence of rolling the dice for a pass or miss.

Casino Craps

Craps as played in a Las Vegas casino is known as "Bank Craps." That is, the house banks the entire game and players cannot make side bets among themselves. The casino takes all bets and runs the game according to a definite set of house rules.

The game itself is played on a rectangular table approximately 3½ feet wide by 12 feet long, with the playing surface about 12 inches below the raised sides. The tops of the sides are grooved to make it easy for the player to store his chips. The table layout is symmetrical and provides two identical betting areas with a common center area for proposition bets.

Craps Table Layout

At first look, a craps table layout appears quite complicated. After a thorough examination, you will see that it is not so intricate as it appears because all craps table layouts in Las Vegas contain the following marked areas:

Pass Line. Any wagers placed in this area bet that the shooter is going to "pass." If the shooter makes a natural on his first roll, or throws his point before making a 7, he wins for all pass line bettors. If the shooter throws a craps (1–1 or 1–2) or "sevens out" before repeating his point, he loses for all pass line bettors. The house pays even money (1 to 1) on all winning pass line bets. By the way, the pass line is generally called the "front line" by inveterate gamblers and casino personnel.

The only time you should place a bet on the pass line is before the come-out, or first, roll for a new point. It is a mistake to make a wager on this line while the shooter is attempting to make his point since you lose the opening chance of winning on a 7 or 11. Most times, one of the dealers will inform you of your error. However, you should check whether a shooter is coming out with a new

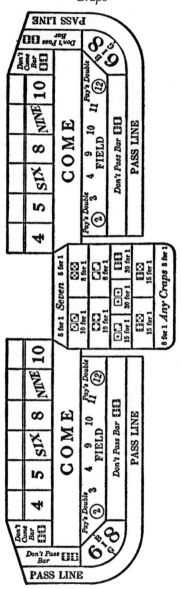

Craps table layout.

point or not by noting the marker, or puck as it is called, in front of the dealer. If the shooter is coming out, the puck will be off the layout and will have "off" written on the top of it. When the shooter is trying for his point, the puck is on the point number with the "on" end showing.

Don't Pass Line. When placing a bet in this section—often called the "back-line"—you are wagering that the shooter is going to lose. If the shooter throws a 2 or 3, or "sevens out" before repeating his point, you and back-line bettors win. If the shooter makes a natural on his first roll, or throws his point before tossing a 7, he and his back-liners lose. The house pays even money on all winning don't pass line bets.

On the don't pass section of the layout, you will note the word "bar" and two dice showing 12. This means that when betting on the back-line, should a double six come up, the bet is off; neither the house nor the players win. It is a standoff, push or tie. You may leave your bet there or remove it as you please, but there is no payoff. Don't pass wagers are made before the come-out roll.

Come. This is one of the most interesting features of Craps. Here is where you can have your own private game against the house. Let us say, for example, that when you enter the game the shooter point is 9. Before his next roll you place your bet on come. On this roll, the shooter throws out an 8. Eight then becomes *your* point. The dealer then moves your bet to 8 in the boxes above the come line. This means that you want the shooter to make an 8 before he makes a 7. If he does, you win; if he does not, you lose. When the come bet is won, it is returned to the come line and is paid off. You should be alert to remove any portion of your bet and winnings as desired before the next roll. Remember that the point for each come bet is separate from the pass line wager and is not affected by the pass line action.

Actually, you can place a bet on the come line on every roll except when a *new* shooter makes his first roll. In this case, the pass line essentially means the same as the come line. On subsequent rolls, however, you can no longer place a bet on the pass line but may make come bets. In reality, a come bet is almost the same as a pass line bet, because on the first roll for come bets as the first loss for line bets, 7 and 11 are winners, 2, 3, and 12 are losers.

Whenever your come bet points are repeated, you win. The odds (1 to 1) are the same, too.

Don't Come. The don't come area is reverse of the come section and the same rules apply as on the don't pass bets, including bar 12. As with the come bet, the first roll after you place your wager in the don't come box is your own personal game, regardless of what is happening on the rest of the table. If the dice show 2 or 3, you are a winner; if 7 or 11 come up, you are a loser; and in the case of 12, you have a standoff with the house. If a point is made, the dealer will place your bet in the back section of the box numbers, signifying that you are a back-liner. If a 7 is rolled before the point is repeated, you win; otherwise you lose. Actually both don't come and don't pass bettors are wagering that the shooter is going to lose. The house pays even odds to don't come winners. While pass and don't pass bets cannot be withdrawn after the come-out, come and don't come wagers can be removed at any time before the roll.

It is interesting to note that when a player bets along with the shooter, it is called a "right" bet. When he bets against the shooter, it is a "wrong" bet. In Craps, the terms "right" and "wrong" have nothing to do with ethics or morals, nor does it mean that a player has guessed right or wrong, so far as winning is concerned. "Right" and "wrong" apply strictly to the type of bet —with the shooter or against him.

Field. When you play the field, you bet on 2, 3, 4, 9, 10, 11 or 12 being rolled. Most casinos pay double on 2 and 12; even money on the other numbers. A few layouts substitute 5 for 4 in the field. A field wager, of course, is a one-roll bet. This means that your wager rides in the field for *only* one roll. That is, each roll is a deciding roll; you win if any of the field numbers appear, or lose if any other number shows.

Big 6 or 8. Here, you simply put your bet on one or the other. If your number (either 6 or 8) comes up before a 7, the house pays even money. Big 6 or 8 are not one-roll bets.

Any 7. When you bet in this section, you are saying that the next roll will be a 7, otherwise you lose. This is a one-roll proposition and the house pays 5 for 1 (4 to 1).

Any Craps. You are betting that 2, 3 or 12 comes up on the next roll of dice. This is also a one-roll bet and the house pays 8 for 1 (7 to 1).

Hard Ways. These are long shots, exact combinations you bet on to come up—namely 2–2, 2–1, 3–3, 4–4, 5–5, 5–6, 6–6. While this is not a one-roll bet, you win only if the numbers come up as such. You lose if the same number comes up any other way—or if 7 comes up. The odds are not uniform for all hard way proposition bets, but the payoff in *most* casinos are as follows:

Combinations	Payoff
1–1; 6–6	30 for 1 (29 to 1)
6–5; 2–1	15 for 1 (14 to 1)
3–3; 4–4	10 for 1 (9 to 1)
2–2; 5–5	8 for 1 (7 to 1)

In the preceding information on payoffs, you note that we used both the words "for" and "to." This is one of the psychological tricks of the casino management. There is a very big difference between stating odds on the basis of "for" instead of "to." The meaning of odds of 30 for 1 is that, on winning, the payoff is 30 units including your initial bet. You are thus receiving odds of 29 to 1. In a similar manner 15 for 1 is 14 to 1; 8 for 1 is 7 to 1; and 5 for 1 is 4 to 1. In practice, the original bet is left on the layout unless you request its return, and the payoff is on the "to" basis. Most craps tables in Las Vegas are marked with "for."

Casino Craps Play

On the player's side of the table you will find a casino employee known as a stickman. It is his primary job to return the dice to the shooter after each roll. He also calls out the dice roll result and places the proposition bets. Some even act as a barker of sorts calling out the proposition bets, because these wagers have a very high house advantage and account for the major portion of the house winnings. On the opposite side of the table, in a restricted area known as the "pit," are the two dealers, one for each end of the table, and a boxman. (When play is heavy, two boxmen may be employed to speed up the game.) The dealer's prime task is to make change from cash to chips, and to collect and pay off bets on his end of the table. The other dealer provides the same function at the other half of the layout. The boxman is the final authority at the table. He carefully follows the game play, handles all called bets that are not marked on the layout, and is the arbitrator if any disputes arise.

Before the first roll of the dice by the shooter—called a *come-out roll*—bets are made by placing the wagers on layouts. As a rule, $1 is the minimum at Las Vegas Strip casinos, while downtown a minimum can be as low as 10 cents.

The stickman begins the action by offering several dice to the shooter who selects two dice. The shooter then throws the dice toward the opposite end of the table so that they bounce off the backboard, and the outcome of the roll is determined by the total of the face-up sides of the dice. The reason the stickman requests that the dice hit the backboard is so that there is no possibility that the fall of the dice can be controlled. It is extremely difficult for an expert to control the dice even if the backboard is not hit; but this caution is often made by the casino personnel because other players feel somewhat cheated if a losing roll does not follow the proper procedure. In most casinos, however, the toss is still considered legal if it does not hit the backboard.

Should the casino personnel be suspicious of a controlled roll, they might call "no dice" or "no roll," if the shooter does not hit the backboard. But only the stickman or a dealer can make the call and they do so under only very unusual situations. The term "no dice" means that there will be no decision on the roll in question. Incidentally, when one or both the dice leave the table during a roll, we have an automatic "no dice" situation. Also the dice that drop off the table are removed from the game. The reason for doing this is to minimize the possibility of introducing biased dice into the game. Of course, the casino can change the dice at any time, but seldom do, even during a player's unusually long "hot" streak. The shooter can ask for new dice at any time and his request will usually be honored.

If the shooter on the come-out roll throws a 2, 3, or 12, the results are a loss for the pass line bettors and a win for the don't pass wagers. A roll of 7 or 11 on the come-out is a win for those with their money on the pass line and loss for back-liners. A roll of 4, 5, 6, 8, 9 or 10 results in designation of a point, and the layout is marked with a puck to indicate the shooter's point.

After the designation of a point, the pass and don't pass line bets can no longer be changed because the point is in action. The shooter then tosses the dice until he tosses his point or a 7. Although there are many bets (the come, don't come and one-rollers) that can be made on each throw of the dice, the pass and don't pass line bets are only affected by the toss of the point number or a 7. If the point is thrown first, this is a winning roll and an amount equal to the pass line bet is paid by the dealer by placing it next to the initial wager. The shooter retains the dice and is free to change his bet in any manner he wishes, except that a minimum bet must be made to continue shooting. The next roll would be a new come-out roll.

If the shooter tosses a 7 before making his point, he sevens out (pass line bettors lose while back-liners win) and has to give up the dice. The player immediately to his left is then given the opportunity to shoot. Thus, when joining a casino game with several open positions, refrain from selecting one that would make you the next shooter. Common courtesy would dictate that you choose a spot in the general area to the right of the shooter. There is nothing more irritating to a player at the table than to have a new player squeeze in between him and the shooter just as he was about to be the next shooter.

Proposition, field, come and don't come bets, as previously stated, can be made at any time. The latter two bets are often confusing to the newcomer to Craps. Actually, the bet is made in the same manner as the pass line, by placing the wager in the come area, and the roll following the bet becomes the come-out roll for this wager. This bet can be made by anyone at the table, including a new arrival who otherwise would have to wait until there was a decision on the current point.

After making a bet on the come, you follow the same rules of Craps which apply to a come-out roll—the 2, 3, and 12 craps result in a loss, 7 and 11 naturals are a win. For a number 4, 5, 6, 8, 9, and 10 roll, this becomes the box number for this bet and is paid off as a winner if the particular number is tossed before a 7, and is lost if a 7 is tossed first. A come bet can be made on every roll except for the table come-out roll, at which the bet is made on the pass line. On the shooter's sevening out, the last come bet is a winner, since it is a "natural" for this bet.

When the dice are in play, make certain that your hands are kept away from the playing area. For the dice to strike a player's hands is often considered "bad" luck by many players, and to have the dice turn up an unfavorable 7 or craps at that time may result in a silent comment or two not exactly favorable to your personal well being.

Of course, if you are like most Craps players, your "big" moment comes when you are the shooter. Remember that a good Craps shooter will always toss the dice down the center of the table with enough force to strike the opposite backboard. This type of toss will minimize the possibility of hitting the dealers' hands, or of having the dice end up behind the dealer's supply of chips. While it may be a legal toss, your failure to hit the backboard with the dice is particularly irritating to some of the other players, especially on an unfavorable roll.

The Importance of Odds, Percentages, and Betting

Let us see how the odds and percentages of Craps are determined. First, there are 36 ways in which a pair of dice can come to rest, and in all cases the total will be some number from 2 to 12. The table below shows these eleven numbers and the number of possible combinations that form each number.

2 can be made in only one way: 1–1
3 can be made in two ways: 2–1, 1–2
4 can be made in three ways: 2–2, 3–1, 1–3
5 can be made in four ways: 2–3, 3–2, 4–1, 1–4
6 can be made in five ways: 5–1, 1–5, 4–2, 2–4, 3–3
7 can be made in six ways: 3–4, 4–3, 5–2, 2–5, 6–1, 1–6
8 can be made in five ways: 5–3, 3–5, 6–2, 2–6, 4–4
9 can be made in four ways: 6–3, 3–6, 5–4, 4–5
10 can be made in three ways: 6–4, 4–6, 5–5
11 can be made in two ways: 6–5, 5–6
12 can be made in one way: 6–6
Total: 36 Combinations

Knowing that there are thirty-six ways of making these eleven numbers and also how many ways each individual number can be made, it is not difficult to obtain the correct odds on all points and off-numbers. This is done simply by figuring the number of ways the *point* can be made as against the six combinations by which 7 can be made. The following chart gives the odds against passing or making the point. The correct odds are also shown in terms of money bets.

4 can be made in 3 ways, 7 in 6 ways—odds are 2 to 1 against the shooter
5 can be made in 4 ways, 7 in 6 ways—odds are 3 to 2 against the shooter
6 can be made in 5 ways, 7 in 6 ways—odds are 6 to 5 against the shooter
8 can be made in 5 ways, 7 in 6 ways—odds are 6 to 5 against the shooter
9 can be made in 4 ways, 7 in 6 ways—odds are 3 to 2 against the shooter
10 can be made in 3 ways, 7 in 6 ways—odds are 2 to 1 against the shooter

As was stated in Chapter 2, it is most important to know the odds. Actually, the major difference between the average player and an expert is the failure of non-professionals to take into account the actual odds on the various bets as opposed to the odds he receives from the house. Bets which pay off at much less than the correct odds are the quickest way to make a player's bankroll nose-dive. But, rather than bore you with page after page of mathematical calculations, we have compiled the following table that gives you the essential information that you need to know about Craps' odds and percentages.

Bet	Chances Against		Chances For	House Pays	Percentage in House's Favor	House's Percentage on $5 Bet*
Pass Line	251	to	244	1 to 1	1.414	$.07
Come	251	to	244	1 to 1	1.414	.07
Don't Pass Bar 6–6	976	to	949	1 to 1	1.402	.07
Don't Come Bar 6–6	976	to	949	1 to 1	1.402	.07
Field (2, 3, 4, 9, 10, 11, 12)	20	to	16	1 to 1	11.111	.56
Field (2, 3, 4, 9, 10, 11, 12. Double on 2 or 12)	380	to	340	1 to 1	5.263	.26
Field (2, 3, 5, 9, 10, 11, 12)	19	to	17	1 to 1	5.555	.27
Big 6	6	to	5	1 to 1	9.090	.45
Big 8	6	to	5	1 to 1	9.090	.45
Any 7	5	to	1	4 to 1	16.666	.83
Any Craps	8	to	1	7 to 1	11.111	.56
Hard Way, 4 or 10	8	to	1	7 to 1	11.111	.56
Hard Way, 6 or 8	10	to	1	9 to 1	9.090	.45
11 or 3	17	to	1	14 to 1	16.666	.83
2 or 12	35	to	1	29 to 1	16.666	.83

* The Bank's edge on a $5 wager given in cents has, in each case a plus fraction which we have omitted.

From noting the percentages in the table, it is obvious that you should stay away from proposition and field bets. While they are *very* popular, they are *most* unprofitable for the player. Sometimes a so-called "high roller" will make a 7 or "any craps" bet as insurance against the come and pass line bets. A typical application of the any Craps insurance bet is as follows:

The bettor has $500 on the pass line and wants to assure not losing the bet in the case of any craps. He then places $75 on any craps. Should a craps come up, he would lose his pass line bet but be paid off $525 on the any craps bet, giving him a $25 profit plus the same bet on the pass line of $500, and on the previous any craps of $75. However, a knowledge of the mathematics of the game would show him that he is paying an 11.1 per cent premium on the $75 bet, or $8.20 for a single roll. By comparison the pass line bet of $500 has a house advantage of only $7, considering even the craps possibilities.

The same high roller often will insure himself against a 7 on a come-out roll when he has significant bets on the numbers via previous come wagers. Again, this is a poor bet because of the 16.7 per cent house advantage on the any 7 proposition.

Craps is not a game for the faint-hearted; there is no place for so-called insurance in the game. First, betting against yourself merely reduces the effective win possibility; and, secondly, the cost of this so-called insurance is so high as to be prohibitive.

Bets not on the Layout

There are several bets that are available to Craps players which do not appear on the table layout and are handled by the dealer or boxman. Some of them such as the "three-way craps" and "horn-bet" are one-roll sucker wagers that should be stayed away from. But, for the uninitiated, a "three-way craps" bet is a one-roll affair in which you are betting the same as "any craps," but in this case you are betting at least one chip on each of the crap numbers and your payoff, rather than being 7 to 1, is 14 to 1 if three is thrown and 29 to 1 if either 2 or 12 is rolled. In other words, three-way-craps is merely a simple way of telling the dealer you want a $1 bet on each of the three craps numbers. The house percentage on such a bet is 16.7 per cent.

The horn-bet is another 16.7 per cent house advantage wager. To place it, give the dealer four chips and call "horn-bet." This means that you are wagering one chip on each of the craps numbers plus 11. If 3 or 11 appears, you will be paid 14 to 1; if 2 or 12 comes up, the payoff is 29 to 1. This is a one roll bet and can be placed at any time.

Place Bets

The most popular of the non-layout wagers are the place bets and box numbers. On all layouts in Las Vegas, you will find the numbers 4, 5, 6, 8, 9, and 10 in boxes. These are called, "Place Numbers" or "Box Numbers." While these numbers are primarily for come-bets and don't-come bets (see page 44), they are used in many casinos for place bets. In most Las Vegas establishments, place wagers go on the line that separates the "do" and "don't" spaces for point numbers on the come and don't-come bets, or on the line in front of the numbered point box. Place bets can be made at any time and you do not have to wait for a new shooter.

To make a place bet, you merely hand your chips to the dealer and say "Place four," or "Place nine." You may call any number appearing in the boxes. This means you are betting that your number, in any combination, will appear before a 7. Here are the odds:

Point	Actual Odds	Correct Odds	Percentage in House's Favor	House's Percentage on $5 Bet
6 or 8	7 to 6	6 to 5	1.515	.08
5 or 9	7 to 5	7½ to 5	4.000	.20
4 or 10	9 to 5	10 to 5	6.666	.33

Be sure to memorize the "actual odds" figure because to get full advantage of them you must bet the exact amount to get the full payoff. For example, if you bet on 8, you must bet $6 for the house to pay off at $7. If you wagered $5, you would not be taking full advantage of the odds because, on a $5 bet, the odds would be a fraction of a dollar and casinos cannot take time to make such payoffs. That is, since the Strip casinos will not pay fractions of a dollar, you must make place bets on the numbers 4, 5, 9 or 10 in increments of five in order to have full advantage of the odds. If you bet on a 6 or 8, you should wager in units of six.

Many observers of a Craps game are confused when they see a player receive less than the amount he won. This is easily explained. The player wants to "press" his place bet, which means increasing it after a win. Therefore, when a player wins $9 on a $5 place bet on 4 or 10 and wants to "press" it, the dealer will put a $5 chip on top of the one already working and hand the player the $4 difference. The player now has a $10 place bet on which he may win $18.

When making bets that are off the craps table layout, the verbal wager is in play if it is repeated by the dealer. He will call "no bet" if in his judgment the bet call is too late for the roll in process. If the wager is accepted, you are expected to produce the chips necessary to cover the bet that you made. As a matter of fact, many craps table layouts have the words "no call bets accepted" on them. This refers, not so much to verbally announcing your bets or your intention of making them, which is sometimes necessary, but to calling out bets without producing the money or chips and letting go of it to signify that you are taking a risk. If you put more down on the table or hand more to the dealer than an announced bet actually requires, you will be paid off the proper amount for your win on the announced bet.

Buy Bets

Another way of wagering on a particular number in addition to place bets is the buying of a number. In buying a number the player pays an added 5 per cent commission on his bet of any of the box numbers (4, 5, 6, 8, 9, or 10) to obtain the correct odds on the number. This commission, which is charged against the short end of the bet and is payable at the time you make the bet, is called *vigorish* and, needless to say, is very helpful to the well-being of casino proprietors. You can see what we mean by looking at the following table:

Point	Buy Bet Odds Under 5% Commission	Percentage in House's Favor	House's Percentage on $5 Bet
4 or 10	2 to 1	4.761	.25
5 or 9	3 to 2	4.761	.25
6 or 8	6 to 5	4.761	.25

Buy bets, like the other place bets, are removable any time before a decision is reached on them. If you decide to drag down your bet, both the amount of the bet and the prepaid commission will be returned to you. The house earns that 5 per cent commission only when there is winning or losing action on your bet. To obtain full value from the commission, the short end of your bet should be for not less than twenty times the amount of the commission. Since the Strip casinos do not acknowledge fractions of a dollar, this means that lowest buy bet that can be effectively made in these establishments is $20 (5 per cent of $20 is $1; the $1 is the commission). If you are wagering large amounts the 5 per cent commission presents no special problem, but for the average player it makes a buy bet almost untouchable. But do not feel bad. Buy bets, if they are wagered, should be made only on the points 4 and 10. The regular place bets on 5, 6, 8 or 9 cost you less. Actually, the only buy or place bets that make any sense at all are *placing* the 6 or 8 which has a house advantage of 1.515 per cent. The other place or buy bets, which range from 4.000 to 6.666 per cent house advantage, are considered "sucker" or foolish wagers.

Incidentally, many Las Vegas casinos, at present, do not allow or else frown upon "placing" or "buying" back-line bets. In establishments which permit these "wrong" bets, you can see by the following table, that for the most part, they could be said to be sucker wagers that should be avoided.

Place Bets to Lose	Percentage in House's Favor	House's Percentage on $5 Bet
House takes 11 to 5 on 4 or 10*	3.030	.15
House takes 8 to 5 on 5 or 9	2.500	.12
House takes 5 to 4 on 6 or 8	1.818	.09

Buy Bets to Lose (5% Charge) *

House takes 2 to 1 on 4 or 10	2.439	.12
House takes 3 to 2 on 5 or 9	3.225	.16
House takes 6 to 5 on 6 or 8	4.000	.20

* This means that the house is taking the bet and is on the long end of the odds; you must thus put up eleven units to win the house's five.

Taking the Odds

This betting option, often called "free or full" odds, is seldom used by beginning Craps players and is rarely mentioned in any of the free literature distributed by the casinos. The reason for the latter is quite obvious; the house has no advantage at all in these bets since the odds are mathematically correct. That is, point 6 or 8 pays 6 to 5; point 5 or 9 pays 3 to 2; and point 4 or 10 pays 2 to 1. There is no marking on the craps table layout indicating how the taking of odds is possible. Here is how it is done:

When the shooter comes out on the point, practically all the Las Vegas casinos allow the players who have previously placed bets on the pass line to then make a second wager, usually equal to the flat or original bet, that the shooter will make his point. (Some Craps tables whose limit is $300 or $500 will allow only $150 or $250 respectively as a free maximum-limit odds bet, even though the front-line wager is greater.) If the point is made, the player receives even money for his original bet and the true odds on his secondary bet.

As with the place bet, it is important to memorize the free odds so that you receive the exact amount of your payoff. For instance, the 5 and 9 should be in increments of two so that the wager can be paid at 3 to 2. The 4 and 10 may be wagered in increments of one so the house pays 2 to 1. The 6 and 8 should be in increments of five, so that the bettor can be paid 6 to 5. In the latter case, you cannot take the odds for a flat bet of $1 or $2, but most casinos will allow you to make a $5 odds bet for a $3 or $4 flat bet.

To illustrate a wager when taking the odds, let us suppose a shooter rolls a 9 for his point. If you have made a bet of $5 on the pass line, you may take the odds with a wager of $2, $4 or $6. The procedure is to set the free odds bet in back of the pass line wager and call out to the dealer that you are taking the odds. If the shooter makes his point, you will receive even money for your pass line wager and 1½ times the full odds wager. (The point 9 pays the true odds of 3 to 2.) In other words, to take the odds, you must first place a flat bet on the pass line. Then, after the come-out toss in which the point is established, you have the option of making a second bet at the true odds. If the shooter sevens out you lose both bets. If he makes his point, you win both bets.

In most casinos you can also take full odds on flat come bets *after* your come number has been established. Taking the odds on a come number is made by placing the amount of the odds bet before the dealer after a particular come roll on which you have made a flat come bet and stating "odds" or "full odds." He will then place your come bet on the come number with the odds wager somewhat displaced to indicate that this portion of your bet should be paid off at full odds. Remember to be patient with the dealer when taking the odds, but do not be timid about attracting his attention. There may be other players competing for his attention, too. The dealer is not a mind reader and he will welcome your telling him what the money is for when you hand it to him.

On paying off a winning roll on a previous bet, the dealer will generally put the original come bet and odds wager in the come area. Your payoff for your flat come bet will be placed next to the come wager and the full odds payoff will be found next to the odds bet, with the bonus portion easily noted.

There is a *general* house policy in most of Vegas' casinos that all odds bets (including place and buy wagers) are "off" on the come-out toss. You can, if you wish, have your free odds bets in play even on the come-out by stating to the dealer that your wager is "on" or "working." Since there is no mathematical advantage or disadvantage either way, the decision as to whether the odds bet is "on" or "off" on the come-out roll is a matter of personal preference. Remember that you are free to change your mind at any time and call the odds off, reduce the size of the free odds wager, or remove it completely. Since there is no house advantage to these bets, the casinos are not particularly anxious for you to take the odds.

Taking the odds, as was stated previously, is restricted to

players who have flat bets. Very rarely an exception may be made in the case of one player staking another (furnishing the money for his gambling) or perhaps a husband and wife, playing at the same table, who may be considered as one for betting purposes. Under the circumstances, for example, the husband could take the odds in connection with his wife's line bet if she neglected to do so herself. If there are relatively few players at a table and the dealer gives his consent to this, it is all right. Do not, however, attempt it or even ask to do it at a very busy table, because the dealers have enough to do and think about already without becoming involved in attempting to remember who is wagering for someone else.

As we have said many times in this book—and it cannot be over-emphasized—the only way to gamble effectively is to keep the house advantage to a minimum. This can best be accomplished by limiting your bets to the pass line and come spaces only and always taking the free odds. Under the free odds condition, the house edge falls to 0.848 per cent—by far the best regular bet in the entire casino. At one time a few casinos in Las Vegas allowed you to take "double" free odds which lowered the house advantage to 0.606 per cent. The term "double odds" refers to the allowance of free odds bet of twice the magnitude of the associated flat wager. Unfortunately, for the gambler, double odds are a thing of the past in Las Vegas. But, in any case, keep Sam Landy's fine advice in mind: "Always take the odds . . . even if you go broke."

Laying the odds

If you are a back-line bettor, you must lay odds instead of taking odds. In this case, you are wagering that the point will not be made, since you are betting against the dice. If the shooter sevens out, you will be appropriately paid at 1 to 2, 2 to 3, or 5 to 6, depending on what the point is.

It is important again, of course, to make your bets in the correct increments. That is, the wager should be in increment of six for the 6 and 8 to pay 5 for 6. For the 4 and 10, the bet should be in increments of two to pay 1 for 2. For 5 and 9, the wager should be in increment of three to be paid 2 for 3. In most casinos that permit laying odds it is usually possible to make larger bets on the odds than what you have on the back line, larger in an amount such that, if you win, the payoff to you equals your flat or original wrong bets.

Let us suppose you have placed a $5 bet on the don't pass section and the shooter throws 10. In casinos where you are permitted to lay odds, you may place an additional bet outside the layout behind the don't pass line. Since the shooter threw a 10 in our example, you must bet in increments of two, up to $10. If the shooter sevens out before he makes a 10, you receive even money for the lnie wager and one-half the odds bet. That is, if you lay the odds of $10, you would receive even money for your original $5 wager and another $5 for the $10 you laid.

The back-line bettor enjoys an equally low percentage bet (0.832 per cent). For this reason, if you bet the don't pass line or don't come, it is always wise to lay the odds.

In closing this chapter on Craps, it is safe to say that the best buys in the game are the pass, come, don't pass, don't come bets and to take or lay the full free odds. Playing these bets and the avoidance of all proposition bets is by far the best way to play, and is the mark of an expert player. Playing in such a manner, even at low betting levels, coupled with proper money management, makes you an intelligent player and more dangerous to the casino than the "high rollers." Do not be intimidated by the action of these players; most of them do not know how to play the game properly. The amount of money you wager does not make you a better or worse player; the technique of your play determines your classification. This may be hard to believe, but it can be vouched for by the casino management personnel as being completely true.

4

♠

Blackjack, or Twenty-One

"Hit me and make it good" is the cry as one to six people play to beat the dealer and woo fickle fate. Of the thousands of card games, Blackjack, or Twenty-One, as it is more correctly known, is one of the easiest to understand and perhaps the most exciting to play. It is usually considered the second-best gambling buy for the "average" player in Las Vegas.

The Basic Elements of the Game

The first step in mastering Blackjack—or any game, for that matter—is a thorough understanding of the rules governing its play. While many people have played Blackjack at home with their friends where "home rules" have applied, the average person on his first visit to a Las Vegas casino is generally somewhat bewildered by the rules. In addition to this, confusion is often heightened by the fact that Blackjack rules vary slightly from casino to casino. Thus it is always a good idea to check with the dealer regarding interpretation of house rules before starting play. As to the play itself, here are the basic essentials:

Layout

Blackjack is played on a semi-circular table covered with green felt. During the course of play, the dealer stands behind the table

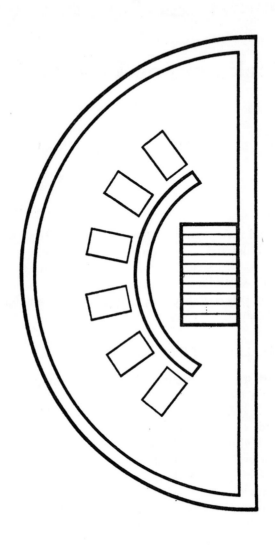

Blackjack table layout.

while the players sit opposite him. There are usually spaces for six players, although a few casinos employ five and others seven spaces. On the table in front of each player is a square, circle, or other design on which the players place their wagers. All bets must be placed on or in this designated area before the start of *each* deal.

Cards

Blackjack is played with a regular deck of playing cards in which the card values are as follows:

Ace—counted as either 1 or 11.
King, Queen, Jack—counted as 10.
2 through 10—counted at their numerical identities, or at face value.

Object of the Game

In Blackjack, you and your fellow players attempt to obtain a higher total card count than the dealer—he is considered to be the house—by attaining 21 or as close to 21 as possible without exceeding that sum. At your proper turn of play and at your own discretion, you may stand pat or draw one or more cards in an attempt to better your card count. Should your total card count go over 21, you have *busted* and have lost your bet. You must turn your cards face up at once, and the dealer will immediately pick them up. If your card count is closer to 21 than the dealer or should he exceed 21, of course, you win.

Betting Limits

You must make your wager before receiving your first card by placing the amount of your bet on the spot reserved for it. The casino places both a minimum and maximum limit on what you can bet. On the Las Vegas Strip, the minimum bet limit is usually $1, while the maximum ranges from $100 to $500. There are times, especially when high rollers, or big spenders, are present, that the house will raise the maximum to $1,000. If you like your Blackjack action small and cannot stand the $1 minimum, chances are good that a game with a minimum as low as 25 cents may be found in downtown Vegas. Information pertaining to the limits is supposed to be posted at the table or on a sign prominently displayed close to it, but a few casinos are somewhat delinquent in publicizing this important information.

Methods of Dealing

While one to four standard fifty-two-card decks may be employed in the game, a single deck is still the common practice in most Las Vegas casinos. The use of double and multi-decks result in a slightly higher house percentage and their use has been threatened by the casino owners for some time.

Before play begins, the dealer shuffles the cards and places them in front of the player whose turn it is to cut. The cut is usually made by inserting a Joker face up into the deck at any place he chooses and the dealer completes the cut at that point. Some casinos permit the standard cutting procedure used in most card games. But whatever method of cutting is employed, the deck's top card is "burned," or placed face up against the bottom of the pack. In most casinos, the dealer never looks at the burned card, nor does he show it to the players. However, if you wish to know the card, it is permissible to ask. It is optional with the dealer whether or not he will reveal the burned card. Most pit bosses stand behind their dealer's decision on this matter.

A single deck is either held in the dealer's hand or laid on the table layout as the cards are being dealt out. While it is customary for the dealer to pick up the "used" cards at the end of each hand of play and place them below the burned card, a few casinos now have their dealers stack the used cards face down on a designated place on the layout. Where this method is employed, it is not necessary to burn a card and thus the full fifty-two cards may be used. For when the top card is burned the last card in the deck cannot be used either and the play of the game is confined to only the fifty cards in-between. That is, when, during play, the dealer reaches the card ahead of the burned card, he re-shuffles the cards in his hand and offers them to a player to cut, again burning a card before restarting play. Incidentally, with either method, the dealer has the option to shuffle the cards at any time between hands.

Where two or more decks are employed, an open-faced box, or *shoe*, is used to hold the cards. This dealing box remains on the table and cards are withdrawn from it one at a time by the dealer. The used cards can either be placed in back of the movable partition in the shoe or stacked face down on layout, depending on how the casino prefers this detail to be handled. A burned card is generally used to mark the need for a shuffle. Actually, the shoe is now being used in a few casinos even for a single deck and there has been some talk that Nevada Gaming Commission *may* require a dealing box to be used on all games of Blackjack in the state.

At present there is a difference as to how single and multi-decks are dealt. In the case of the former, the first two cards given to the players are delivered face down, while those dealt from multi-deck shoe are generally turned face up. (In some of the casinos on the Strip where multi-decks are employed, the cards are dealt in the same manner as a single deck.) Under either arrangement, the dealer's first two cards are dealt one face up and second face down. All additional cards to either the players or dealer are dealt face up.

The Play of the Game

Once the cards are dealt, the dealer offers each player the option of staying pat with the first two cards or drawing more. There are, however, two exceptions to this basic procedure:

1. If the dealer's face-up, or showing, card is an Ace or a 10-value card, he will look at his down, or hole, card without revealing it to the players. Should the dealer have a *natural* 21 (Ace and 10-value card), or Blackjack, he will turn over his down card and will collect all bets except those by players who have Blackjack and standoff, or tie, him.

2. If the dealer's showing card is an Ace, he will offer "insurance" to each of the players prior to looking at his hole card. This gives each player the opportunity to insure his hand against the possibility of dealer having a natural 21. That is, any player wish-

ing to insure his bet against the dealer having Blackjack must place one-half his original bet in the betting area directly in front of him. When all players have had the chance to make an insurance bet, the dealer then looks at his hole card. If it is a 10-value card, giving him a natural, he then pays all players who made insurance bets 2 to 1 on the amount of their insurance bet and then takes the amount of their original bet. If, however, the dealer does not have Blackjack he collects the amount of the insurance bets only. The advantages and disadvantages of insuring a bet will be discussed later in this chapter.

When the dealer does not hold Blackjack, the player at his extreme left plays first. If the player holds a natural 21, he calls Blackjack and turns his cards up so the dealer can verify the count. The dealer then pays off the player at 3 to 2 odds, or 1½ times the money he has bet. If the player's two cards total less than 21 he may decide:

1. *To stand pat.* He has reached this decision because he is satisfied with his count or fears that a third card may "bust" his hand by making his card total go over 21. He simply says "I stand," "Good," or "I'm O.K." He may also signify that he is standing pat by sliding his cards under the chips he has bet.

2. *To draw one or more additional cards.* This decision is usually reached because the player is not satisfied with the card count. In such a case, he says, "Hit me," or makes a come-on motion with his finger or by scratching the table with his cards. The dealer then gives the player a card off the top of the deck face up and next to his original two cards. If a player wants a fourth, fifth or sixth card he may have it. Thus, when he feels that his count is as good as he can get, he says "I have enough," or makes a stop sign. But, should he go over 21, he must turn his down cards face up immediately and surrender his bet.

The play moves to the player's left, clockwise around the table until each player either stands or busts. If a player should forget to hit a hand he may *not* ask to be hit after the dealer has dealt to the next player. If a down card is accidentally exposed during play, it does *not* invalidate a hand.

In casino Twenty-One, the dealer *always* plays last. Should all players bust, he merely places his own cards face up on the bottom deck (or the designated place on the layout), and deals the next round. If any *active* players remain in the game, the dealer must play his hand as follows:

1. He turns his hole card up, exposing all his cards.

2. If his total count is 16 or less, the dealer must draw a card. He must keep drawing cards until his total is 17 or more.

3. If the dealer's count is 17 or more, he must *stand*—in most major casinos—even if he has a soft 17 (meaning a 17 count using an Ace as 11, plus a six spot). There are still a few clubs in Las Vegas that require a dealer to *hit* on a soft 17. This vital information is usually printed right on the table layout. But, if it is not, be sure to check with the dealer before starting play. It is to the advantage of the player for the dealer to stand on a soft 17.

4. Once the dealer stands, he pays even money for their bets to those players with higher totals than his and collects the bets of those who have a lower count. Ties, or "pushes," between players and dealer are standoffs, with no money changing hands. If the dealer busts, he must pay off at even money to all the players still in the game. But, in any case, the active players should not turn over their cards; this is the task of the dealer. After he flips over the players' cards and verifies the count, the payoff is made.

As you can see, the Blackjack dealer has no choice of action. His decisions as to whether he stays pat or draws are predetermined and are known to the players before play starts. Since all his cards are exposed at his turn of play, the dealer has no opportunity for any departure from the house rules.

Play for the next hand starts almost immediately. That is, for the players wishing to play, bets are made and the deal begun *generally* without re-shuffling the cards. As described earlier, the dealer continues from where the play was interrupted by exhaustion of the cards in his hand or in the shoe. At this point, the dealer shuffles the cards, even in the midst of the play of a hand. Also as previously stated, the dealer has the right to shuffle at *any time* between hands. The player may also request a shuffle between hands. Some dealers comply, while others may refuse. In addition, the player by custom, but not required by house rules, is able to request a new deck whenever he desires. When a new deck is introduced in a game, it is generally spread out face down. This permits the dealer to inspect the backs of the cards for any imperfections that could be used by the players to identify cards when they are face down. Then the cards are spread face up. This gives the players an opportunity to make sure that no cards have been added to or removed from the deck. The dealer can put a new deck into play at any time according to his own discretion.

Betting Options

There are two very important betting options that a player must always consider. They are:

Splitting. If a player is dealt two cards of identical value, he has the option of "splitting" the pair and playing each card as a separate hand. This is done by turning up his cards and by doubling his original wager to cover his twin hands. The dealer then gives him a second card face down on each hand. From this point on, he plays each hand separately, standing or drawing in the normal manner—with several minor exceptions.

First, if a player splits a pair and draws a third card of identical value to the first two, most casinos permit him to split again to form a third hand. The same procedure as described above must be followed.

Another exception is that if a natural 21 results from a split pair the player is paid off at only even money.

And finally, should a player receive a pair of Aces and split them, he receives one card—and only one card—on each Ace. If a split Ace is hit with another Ace, the house rules in most casinos will not allow the player to split for a third time. Again, if a natural should occur, the hand is not considered a Blackjack, but simply a 21.

Doubling Down. While the rules for "doubling down" vary in Las Vegas, most casinos will allow a player to double on any two cards. After the first two cards are dealt, a player, wishing to double down, turns his cards face up and informs the dealer that he desires to double the bet—then doubles his bet. (Incidentally, some casinos do not require an exact doubling of the bet and will permit the adding of any amount up to the original wager.) After the additional wager has been added to the original bet, the dealer gives the player *only* one card face down. The total of the three cards now represents the player's hand—no more cards may be drawn. The correct occasions to double down, as well as when to split pairs, will be explained later in this chapter.

These are the basic elements of Blackjack play. Let us now take a look at finer techniques as viewed by our Las Vegas experts, under the direct co-ordination of Sherlock Feldman, well-known pit boss at the Dunes Hotel.

Blackjack Strategy

Unlike the other casino games, Blackjack was not originally devised with specified odds against the player. It evolved from a home-type card game and was adapted to casino play. For this reason, it is rather difficult to give *exact* house advantage percentage as with the other casino games. Actually, with each card dealt the house percentage varies ever so slightly. But most experts agree that the house percentage against a *good* player is from 2 to 3 per cent. The *smart* player who takes full advantage of all play factors, however, can shave this percentage to *almost* zero. Actually, some mathematicians and gaming theoreticians claim that the house's advantage is *less* than 0.2 per cent when Blackjack is played with computer accuracy. Actually, Blackjack is about the only casino game in which skill plays any part. Let us take a look at some of the advantages that the player has:

1. The player is paid at odds of 3 to 2 when he holds a natural 21.

2. Unlike the dealer, the player can stand or hit on any card count provided he does not exceed 21. That is, at his turn of play he may draw or stand pat.

3. The player is the one who determines the amount of the wager and can increase or lower it as he sees fit within the prescribed casino betting limits.

4. The player may split pairs or double down if the situation appears favorable.

5. In some casinos, the player may play as many hands as there are available betting spaces.

6. The player may count, or "case," the deck. By remembering the cards previously played and exposed, his chances of winning are a great deal better. An expert card-counter once profited by more than $25,000 at a downtown Las Vegas casino because the establishment's boss stubbornly refused to believe that card casing would give a player any degree of an advantage.

7. The player has the opportunity to see one of the dealer's cards and may use this information in determining the play of his hand.

8. The dealer is not interested in the cards the players are holding, since the rule by which he plays—drawing to 16 and standing on all 17—is inflexible. Up until recently, it was thought that this prohibition on the dealer gave the house an advantage in that it relieved the dealer of making individual decisions that could work to the house's disadvantage. Now, electronic computer studies show that this premise may not be completely true. As a matter of fact, the house's only real advantage is that *the dealer plays last*. If it were not for this rule, the player's chances of winning would be as good—maybe better—than the dealer's. The player often will start out with a hand that is potentially better than the dealer's—but if he busts (goes over 21) with it the house collects on the bet it might otherwise have lost. It is also because of this rule that the player who follows the dealer's procedure of hitting all totals to 16 and standing on 17 and higher is doomed to failure. A player that does so incurs a disadvantage of about 6 per cent and this is too high for successful play.

To be a "smart," or educated, Blackjack player you must:

1. Know the basic elements of the game, especially when to hit or stand, and whether or not to split pairs or double down.

2. Case or count the cards that have been drawn from the deck, and which cards have not been played from the pack. This is much more difficult than in other card games such as Bridge and Pinochle since in Blackjack there is no set fashion in which the cards will fall.

3. Know money management—when to wager big and when to bet small.

The Strategy for Hitting and Standing

The only players who win consistently at Blackjack over the long run are those who draw to beat the dealer. All too many players beat themselves by drawing improperly. That is, they take chances which invariably make them bust. The educated player, on the other hand, utilizes the dealer's two major disadvantages—his one card exposed and the house rule's determining his play. For instance, when the dealer's exposed card indicates there is a good chance that he will have to draw and may go bust, the smart player will play so that the chances are that he will not. Thus, the first step in learning to become an "expert" Blackjack player is to know when to stand and when to hit.

For this information, we have tabulated the advice given by the dealers and pit bosses of several major casinos and then compared it to the findings of two computer tests. The results are as follows:

If you have 17 or more, regardless of what the dealer shows, stand pat—do not hit. All too often players with 17 forget this strategy when the dealer's up card is 10, Jack, Queen or King. They are sure that he has a 10-value card in the hole. Thus they will hit and go over. Remember that it is not an easy matter to have a pat hand of from 17 to 20. The chances are less than 1 in 3.

There are three exceptions to this basic rule of standing on 17—all of them have to do with doubling down and splitting. For instance, it is wise to split a pair of 9's, except when the dealer shows a 7, 10 or Ace. Likewise, it is considered good play to double down on a *soft* 17 (Ace-6) when the dealer shows 3, 4, 5, or 6, and hit when 2, 7, 8, 9, 10, or Ace are exposed. Likewise, on a *soft* 18, it is wise to stand if dealer shows 2, 3, 7, 8 or Ace; double down on 4, 5, 6; or hit on a 9 or 10.

If you have 13 thru 16 and the dealer shows 2, 3, 4, 5, or 6, stand pat—do not hit. Any time a player receives a card count of 13 to 16, he is considered to be holding a "stiff," or bad, hand. It is most important in such instances to capitalize on the dealer's inflexible play. For example, let us suppose that the dealer's up card is a 6 and you are holding 13. The dealer's chances of making a count of 17 to 21 are less than 1 to 2, but your hopes of drawing a card which will give you 17 to 21 are even less than that—approximately 2 to 5. It is always better to let the dealer run the risk of busting.

If you have 13 thru 16 and the dealer shows 7 or more, hit. Here is where some of the experts disagreed. While they said that they would hit 14 or 15, about half said no to 16. But when we checked the computer figures, it showed that the chances of the player hitting and busting were about 3 out of 5. It also indicated that if the player did not hit, the dealer's chances of winning were greater than that—3½ out of 5. Thus, it is wise to hit a stiff hand until you have a 17 or better when the dealer shows 7 or higher.

The strategy for soft 13 thru 16 is given on page 73.

If you have 12 and the dealer shows 4 thru 6, stand pat—do not hit. This is another stiff hand that can cause problems for a player. While you can probably think of dozens and dozens of combinations that will permit you to reach 17 to 21 when you have 12, remember they are outnumbered by all the cards which can send you over 21. Of course, do not be afraid to hit this stiff hand if the dealer's up card is 2, 3, 7 or more. As you will see later in this chapter, card casing or counting can be a great help in deciding the play of a stiff hand.

If you have 11, regardless of what the dealer shows, double down. This strategy may cause some consternation among professional Twenty-One gamblers. Until computers came along the general strategy was never to double down on 11 when the dealer had 9, 10, or Ace showing. But now it has proven best to always double down on a card total of 11, double on a total 10 unless the dealer's up-card is 10 or Ace, and double on a total of 9 when the dealer shows 7 or higher. The edge in favor of doubling becomes successively smaller for 10 and 9, and it is not usually advisable to double on 8 or lower. (The computer indicates a *slight* player advantage in doubling down on 8 when dealer shows either a 5 or 6, but most experts frown on this bit of electronic advice and we will go along with them only as a matter of simplicity.) There are numerous instances, however, that will tempt the more adventurous gambler who does not mind bucking a percentage against him if that percentage is not too high. The expert who is accurately casing the deck goes by the actual situation, not by published guides. If he sees that only low cards remain in the deal, he would prefer to play his hand straight and draw as many cards as he wants rather than double down to get stuck with a low final count. Remember that doubling the bet means you can draw only one additional card and if it should be a low one, you have no chance unless the dealer busts. Several casinos in Las Vegas will permit doubling *only* on 10 and 11, so be sure of the house rules before you start play.

How to handle 10 and below. As previously mentioned, it is sometimes wise to double down on 10 and 9. Except for doubling down as noted, it is necessary, of course, to hit low card count until they are raised to at least 12. From then on, follow the advice given earlier for plays of 12, 13 thru 16, and 17 and more.

FREQUENCY OF PLAYING NUMBERS

No.	Ways of Making	No.	Ways of Making
16	23,020	19	72,380
17	37,970	20	102,120
18	51,700	21	171,060

MAKING PLAYING NUMBER WITH 2 CARDS

No.	Ways of Making	No.	Ways of Making
16	102	19	80
17	96	20	136
18	86	21	64

Odds on making 21 with 2 cards	24–1
Odds on getting 16 or better with 2 cards	1.5–1

MAKING PLAYING NUMBER WITH 3 CARDS

No.	Ways of Making	No.	Ways of Making
16	1,344	19	1,680
17	1,488	20	1,894
18	1,580	21	2,052

Odds on making 21 with 3 cards	13.3–1
Odds on getting 16 or better with 3 cards	1.9–1
Odds on overdrawing with 3 cards	2–1

MAKING PLAYING NUMBER WITH 4 CARDS

No.	Ways of Making	No.	Ways of Making
16	5,055	19	9,744
17	6,240	20	11,297
18	7,650	21	12,420

Odds on making 21 with 4 cards	19–1
Odds on getting 16 or better with 4 cards	4.3–1
Odds on overdrawing with 4 cards	1–2

Splitting pairs. There are favorable and unfavorable pair-splitting situations in Twenty-One. For instance it is never smart play to split 10-count cards. A 20 is fairly difficult to obtain in two cards. As you can see in the frequency of playing numbers chart, there are 136 two-card combinations to make 20. The odds are a little over 8½ to 1 against your having 20 with two cards. Not so easy to get 20, is it? The odds against you to have a pair of 5s or 4s are much larger. These are good hands, so why split them? (The only exception to this, according to the computer, is in the case of 4s when the dealer shows a 5. The odds in this instance *slightly* favor splitting.)

There are pairs that should be split, but experts often disagree as to which ones. For instance, one group says always split a pair of 8s, while others contend it best to split them only against a dealer's 2 through 7. The latter group reasons that when you have a pair of 8s and the dealer has 8, 9, 10 or Ace up, you have a bad hand and should just hit your 16. It is a bad hand and you can make it into a good hand. If you should lose it, you are only losing one bet instead of two by splitting.

There are counts that all experts agree on. Aces, for instance, should always be split. There are also cases where there is little doubt about the benefits derived from splitting. As a case in point, 7s are a good split against the dealer's 2 through 8 showing, because 14 is a bad hand and there are thirty-two cards to improve it. For example, you can catch one of sixteen pictures, which will give you 17, one of four Aces which will give you 18, a 2, 3 or 4 which will give you 9, 10, or 11 which will give you a chance to draw a high card for a winning hand. The same reasoning holds good for 6s, except in this case the split should be made only against the dealer's 2 through 7.

Split 2s and 3s when the dealer's up-card is 2, 3, 4, 5, 6 or 7.

Because of the human element of our experts, we will go along with the computer results for splitting given above. But, remember when you have a pair and the chart does not call for a split, just hit the pair and play the hand the way the chart says.

Soft hand play. "Soft" totals and what to do with them usually present some of the most difficult problems for a novice player. Actually, the only thing to remember in playing a soft hand is that the Ace may be counted as 1 or 11 and adjust your card count accordingly. For example, the dealer's up card is a 3, the player hits a soft 15 and draws an 8. His total count is now 13. If he counted the Ace as 11, he would be bust at 23. Thus his hand can no longer be considered "soft" and the player must revert to his standard strategy and stand on a "hard" 13. Any hand not counting an Ace as 11 is called a *hard* hand.

The strategy for hitting, standing, doubling down and splitting just discussed has been summarized in the following table. Committing it to memory is the first step in becoming an educated Blackjack player. Keep in mind, though, "Lady Luck" calls the final turn.

Your Cards	Dealer's Up Card	Your Action
17 or above	All	Stand
13 thru 16	2,3,4,5,6	Stand
	7,8,9,10,Ace	Hit
12	2,3,7,8,9,10,Ace	Hit
	4,5,6	Stand
11	All	Double Down
10	2,3,4,5,6,7,8,9	Double Down
	10,Ace	Hit
9	2,3,4,5,6	Double Down
	7,8,9,10,Ace	Hit
8 or less	All	Hit
Ace, Ace	All	Split
10,10	All	Stand
9,9	2,3,4,5,6,8,9	Split
	7,10,Ace	Stand
8,8	All	Split
7,7	2,3,4,5,6,7,8	Split
	9,10,Ace	Hit
6,6	2,3,4,5,6,7	Split
	8,9,10,Ace	Hit
5,5	All	Hit
4,4	2,3,4,6,7,8,9,10,Ace	Hit
	5	Split
3,3 and 2,2	2,3,4,5,6,7	Split
	8,9,10,Ace	Hit
Ace, 8 or 9	All	Stand
Ace, 7	2,3,7,8,Ace	Stand
	4,5,6	Double Down *
	9,10	Hit

Your Cards	Dealer's Up Card	Your Action
Ace, 6	2,7,8,9,10,Ace	Hit
	3,4,5,6	Double Down **
Ace, 3 thru 5	2,3,7,8,9,10,Ace	Hit
	4,5,6	Double Down **
Ace, 2	2,3,4,7,8,9,10,Ace	Hit
	5,6	Double Down **

* If doubling down is not permitted by house rules, stand.
** If doubling down is not permitted by house rules, hit.

Insurance Bet. The insurance bet, where it is offered, means that the house is willing to lay 2 to 1 when the dealer is showing an Ace that the dealer will *not* have a natural 21. Your bet, from the player's standpoint, is that the dealer *will* get a Blackjack. This is a *poor* bet under most circumstances.

Many old-time Las Vegas "experts" will tell you that when the dealer shows an Ace and you hold a natural, take out insurance. They contend that this is the only time when it pays you to take out insurance, for by doing so you *make certain of winning*. Let us make a mathematical analysis of this statement:

First, let us see what happens if you take out insurance. Assuming that your original bet is $2, this means that you must put up $1 for insurance. Now, if the dealer has a natural, you tie on your own Blackjack, and win $2 on the insurance bet. If the dealer does not have a natural, you win $3 on your Blackjack, but lose your $1 insurance. In either case, your profit is $2.

Now, if you do not take out insurance and the dealer has Blackjack, you have a standoff, which means your profit is zero. But, if he does not have it, your gain is $3. At first blush, it may appear that insurance, when you have a natural, is a good deal. True, the player who insures his Blackjack has about the only *safe* bet in gambling. But computer studies reveal that *less* than ⅓ of the time will both the player and dealer tie. In other words, *more* than ⅔ of the time, the player has the possibility of gaining 1½ to 1. While the old-timers are completely correct in their statement that you are certain to win when insuring your natural, you never receive its *full* value since you are paying off a house advantage of about 8 per cent to insure this win. As a matter of fact, the only players who make good use of insurance bets are those who can case the deck. Say, for example, the dealer shows an Ace and you know that out of twelve cards left in the deck six of them are 10-value cards. In this case, the odds that the dealer will get Blackjack are 1 to 1, but the odds the insurance bet offers you are 2 to 1. By all means, it is wise to take the bet under such circumstances.

Casing the Deck

One of the most valuable adjuncts that any Twenty-One player can have is the faculty of remembering most of the previously exposed cards. The player who does not develop this aptitude to some degree has little chance of beating the house in the long run, no matter how well he plays otherwise. Because the house's favorable advantage varies with the dealing of each card, the smart player also changes his strategy accordingly. The more dealt cards the player can remember, the greater chance he has of making the proper decisions on future hands.

Counting, or casing, the deck has been going on for years, but in recent years such gaming theoreticians as Dr. Allan Wilson, Roger Baldwin, and Dr. Edward Thorp have publicized the fact that this is the only way to beat Blackjack. Unfortunately, most of their methods, while very well-founded, are too complicated and require memorization beyond the range of the average player. In addition, many of their theories are based on a one-player-vs.-dealer situation. In Las Vegas such playing conditions are seldom possible.

You do not have to have a photographic memory or other great skill to be fairly successful in casing the deck. In this book, we are not going to cover any of the expert casing methods, but rather give you a few fundamentals that will help to develop your own method.

If you can keep track of the 10-count cards and Aces, for example, this information will be most beneficial for the double down plays, insurance bets, and for knowing the chances for busting. Remember that one-third of the deck, minus the Aces, are 10-counters. That is, one out of every three cards should be a 10. But, rather than counting the 10s as they are played, devise a method of keeping a running proportion of the number still in the deck. Here is one method that is quite popular in Las Vegas.

Essentially this method of simple casing involves the proportion number of 10s in each hand. When no 10s show in the player's hand, the count is one plus—which indicates that there is one extra 10 left in the deck in proportion to the remainder of the deck. (Remember that the *average* Blackjack hand contains three cards and there are sixteen 10-counters in a deck.) Should there be two 10 counters in a hand, the score is one minus—the one minus indicating that one less 10 remains in proportion to the remainder of the deck. As each hand is turned up, a mental running count is made. A separate mental note is also made of the Aces, but is not included with the 10s. Here are several Blackjack hands that will show how the running count is made:

K, 2, 7 (even)
3, 7, 2, 4 (1 plus)
9, 4, 6 (2 plus)
K, Q (1 plus)
5, A, Q (1 Ace and 1 plus)
10, 2, 10 (even)

7, 4, 5 (1 plus)
K, A (2 Aces and 1 plus)
4, Q, J (even)
J, 3, K (1 minus)
9, 4, 6 (even)
8, 4, A, 9 (3 Aces and 1 plus)

In the first hand, there was a 10-value card (the King); therefore, the running count was even. In the next hand, there were no 10s, so a one plus means an overbalance of 10s in the deck. (An overbalanced deck is often said to be a positive deck, while an underbalanced one is a negative deck.) The following hand had no 10s either, thus there was an overbalance of two plus. The player's 20 in the next hand shows one extra 10 which brings the count to one plus. In the next hand, the Ace is considered separately, while the one 10 leaves the overbalance the same. When the deck is highly positive or the overbalance is high and Ace count low, this is considered the ideal condition for the player because there are more 10s and Aces in proportion left in the deck. This means the chances for a natural 21 are greater. When the deck is highly negative or underbalance is high, it is usually a safe bet to hit a stiff hand.

To become proficient in the proportion count method of card casing, some practice is required. With a standard deck of cards, turn one card over at a time and keep a running count. The casing should end up with an even count, plus four Aces. Once you can go through the deck rapidly without any difficulty, have someone act as a dealer and practice casing the 10s and Aces in actual Blackjack hands. At first, start with two hands (the dealer's and yours). As your counting technique improves, increase the number of hands until you are able to cope with seven (the dealer's and six players'). Learn to spot the 10 count and Aces quickly, since in a casino game the dealer scoops up the cards rapidly.

Continue your practice as near as possible under game conditions. Sometimes, for instance, the cards will all be dealt out before the round has been completed. In such cases, the dealer shuffles the discards and continues dealing. When this occurs, the card count reverts to even 10s and zero Aces. Then recase all exposed cards and start your normal count. But be sure, when the dealer shuffles, to say to yourself, "Even 10s and zero Aces," otherwise the change is easily missed.

With just a little practice, you will be surprised at how proficient you can become in casing 10s and Aces. While this simple method is usually sufficient for the average player, you may wish to expand your casing prowess further. If you do, we suggest reading a book that contains advance techniques. For instance, Donald I. Collver's *Scientific Blackjack* (Arco Publishing Company) describes a procedure fairly similar to the one just described. However, it carries the system further to casing all the cards in the deck. Of course, the ultimate of all card casing methods is detailed in Dr. Thorp's book, *Beat the Dealer*, but it is far too complicated for the occasional Blackjack player. Also, some of his theories and claims are questioned by many of Las Vegas' Blackjack "experts."

A good card caser will always try to locate himself in the seat at the dealer's extreme right—called by the experts "third base"—because it is the best vantage point for keeping track of the exposed cards. Let us say, for instance, that he has a stiff hand with a count 13 after some 32 cards have been played. Of these 32 cards, he observes that fourteen were 10-value ones and three were 9s. With this information in mind, he knows that there are only three cards left in the deck that can bust him, so he will hit a hand that might normally call for him to stand. Thus his position at the table to observe the most number of cards played can be most vital in his play of the game. Also a card caser will want to play at a table that has only a few players, and, better yet, at one where he and dealer meet "head to head." Quite frequently, if house rules permit, a card caser will play more than one hand. In most casinos where this is allowed, a player can bet on an additional hand if there is an unoccupied space, but in some special conditions may be attached. For instance, when the minimum table limit is $1 on a single hand and he wishes to remain at the minimum rate, the second hand would require a $2 bet, or a total bet of $3. But this $3 total minimum on the two hands can be split and, if the player desires, $1.50 may be laid on each. Wagering on a third hand, under similar conditions, calls for a minimum of $5 on the third hand. Again, the wager may be split up any way the player wants just as long as there is at least $1 on each bet and the total comes to $8 or more. In a few casinos the $2 and $5 bets on the second and third hands, respectively, must also be matched by raising the other bets to those amounts. That is, the player has to bet at least $2 on each hand when playing two of them, and at least $5 on each hand when betting on three hands. At the higher minimum tables ($5 and up) there is usually no stipulation on additional hand play, except that you must keep *all* your bets, for each hand played— whether two, three, or more—at the advertised minimum. Remember, the more hands you play, the more control of the card count you have.

The casinos do *everything* to make card casing difficult. When a pit boss suspects a player of casing the deck, he instructs the dealer to reshuffle the deck frequently and not to deal the deck through to the burned card. This, of course, makes counting mor troublesome. If a suspected caser is the only player at the table, the management will generally send in one or two shills to play, or may even "bar" him from the club. With the increasing awareness of the Blackjack player to the value of card casing, several prominent Las Vegas casino executives believe that the use of single deck in their establishment will soon be a thing of the past. The use of multi-decks, dealt in the same manner as a single one, would make casing the cards much more difficult and give them back their house advantage.

Money Management

As with all casino games, money management is important in Blackjack. True, the object of the game is to draw to beat the dealer. But just drawing to beat the dealer will not really let you win. You must bet to beat the house by wagering properly. While wagering the minimum appears to permit you to "string out" a small amount for a period of time, actually it only prolongs the loss of your money. The only way to win at Blackjack, as with all casino games, is to bet to win—when the odds are in your favor.

The most successful method of money management in Blackjack depends on the player's casing the cards and betting heavily in favorable situations. If the deck is "10 and Ace rich" (high plus count), for instance, the odds favor the player and call for a heavy bet. Remember that the "natural" bonus of 50 per cent (3 to 2 odds) is the basic strategy of money management for all smart players. That is, bet more heavily when the probability of obtaining Blackjack is high, and drop out or only bet small amounts at other times. For instance, if the deck has run half way through and no Aces have appeared, then bet heavily. If three Aces have been exposed, however, bet the minimum.

One question many beginners ask the pit bosses is: Can I withdraw a bet already made or change its amount during play? The answer is yes, but under certain *very* specific conditions. If you placed a large bet and then note that the dealer begins to shuffle the cards after your money is down, thus destroying your supposed advantage from card counting, you may withdraw or reduce your bet, if you act quickly. In a single-deck game, once you have been dealt a card, whether you have looked at it or not, your bet as it stands in the hole must remain unchanged except for any permitted additional betting by splitting pairs or doubling down, until a decision is reached on the play in progress. In the multiple-deck game, the first card dealt face up to any player freezes all the initial betting action at that table, including bets by players not yet reached by the dealing. Remember that the educated Blackjack player not only knows how to take every possible advantage in the game, but he must believe fully in the winning psychology of good money control detailed fully in Chapter 2.

Blackjack Machines

Early in 1965, a large number of automatic Blackjack machines were installed in many Las Vegas casinos. The machines have a minimum of 25 cents and a maximum of $5. Here are instructions as they appear on the machines:

1. "Automatic Blackjack" is electronically operated using a full simulated fifty-two card dcek—automatically shuffled and dealt. Play is initiated upon the deposit of a coin, or coins, in any or all denominations of quarters, halves or silver dollars . . . to a limitation of five coins of each denomination.

2. The sequence of the game is in accord with all standard "Blackjack" or "21" games.

3. The player has the option of "hitting or standing" on the hand and score dealt. All scores are numerically indicated immediately.

4. The "dealer" will continue to draw cards automatically until it has a score of 17 or more—at this time the score of the player is compared to the "dealer" and payoff is automatically made according to the score and the amount of the bet made. If the player makes a "Blackjack" he receives *double* (2 to 1) his original bet instead of the usual one and a half payoff.

5. "Automatic Blackjack" is fully approved by the Nevada Gaming Commission. All card dealing is absolutely uncontrolled and based upon chance.

6. Any player, after receiving two or more cards showing a score of 10 or 11 may elect to "double down." Simply press the yellow flashing light button, increase your bet in the same denomination up to double your original bet, press the "hit" button, and you will receive one card only to complete your hand.

The electronically operated machines have several *disadvantages* for the "good" Blackjack player. The cards are reshuffled after each hand, the player cannot split pairs, doubling is limited to 10 or 11, casing of the cards is impossible, and the machine play is slow. For these reasons, it is wise to stay away from one of these machines unless you just wish to waste away a few quarters. Remember that your success in Blackjack all depends on your skill in playing and in managing your bets, and your luck.

Roulette—The Aristocrat of Gambling Games

When most people think of casino gambling, they automatically have Roulette in mind. It is a great favorite on the Continent, particularly among the aristocracy who still look askance at the more plebeian forms of gaming. While not overly popular with men in the United States, Roulette is an overwhelming choice of women because it offers the drama of the unexpected and the exhilaration of big payoffs.

Because of its slow pace and simple rules, Roulette is one of the easiest casino games for the beginning player to enjoy. And because of its low limit, it is one of the few games of chance in Las Vegas which offers a true gambler whose budget is modest an opportunity to play for a long while without making a major investment.

Around the Roulette Table

There are two basic styles of Roulette tables employed in Las Vegas casinos. One is the standard table, which has one betting layout with the Roulette wheel at one end; the other, called the double-end table, has two layouts with the wheel in the center between them.

The layout itself is a multicolored design printed on green baize that covers the players' side of the table and forms the betting section. The main portion of the design is comprised of thirty-six

81

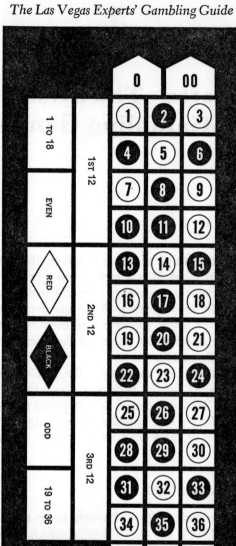

Roulette table layout.

numbered rectangular spaces arranged in three long columns of twelve spaces each. The spaces at the head of the columns are numbered 1, 2, 3, and are nearest the wheel. The numbering continues in sequence across the columns, ending with 34, 35, and 36 at the foot of the columns farthest from the wheel. Directly below these numbers are three blank spaces. A chip placed on one of these indicates that you are betting on the twelve numbers on the long column directly above the space on which the chip rests.

Along one side of the long columns are three rectangular spaces marked: 1st 12, 2nd 12, and 3rd 12. A chip placed on one of these spaces indicates that you are betting on the first 12 numbers, 1 through 12; on the second 12 numbers, 13 through 24; or on the third 12 numbers, 25 through 36. Next to these are six more spaces which read from left to right: 1–18, EVEN, RED, BLACK, ODD, 19–36. Above the three long columns are two spaces with pointed tops containing the figures 0 and 00.

Each number and color on the layout has its counterpart on the wheel. Actually, the Roulette wheel is an elaborate contrivance which inspires confidence by its very appearance. The wheel itself measures about two feet across and is usually made of mahogany, veneered and inlaid with such exotic woods as rosewood, ebony and satinwood, making it quite elegant. At the center of the wheel is a handle which projects upward above a steel pivot on which the wheelhead is perfectly balanced. A simple twist of the handle and the wheelhead will spin smoothly. From the center, the wheel slopes downward to a circle of frets (metal separators) and canoes (pockets). The canoes are colored red and black alternately and bear gold numbers from 1 to 36 inclusive, though not in regular rotation. The exceptions you will find to this are canoes for 0 and 00 which are located opposite each other on the wheelhead and have their gold numbers on a green background.

Around the outside of the numbered circle and its slots, the wheel slants upward forming a circular track within the confines of a high-rimmed bowl. The spinning is done by a dealer, or croupier, who flips a small ½- to ¾-inch-diameter ivory or synthetic plastic ball on the wheel while it revolves. As the spin slackens, the ball is trapped in one of the canoes, or pockets, which represents the winning number.

In most Las Vegas casinos, Roulette is played with chips supplied by the house at the layout. The player sets the value of the chips he uses as well as selecting the color desired. Chips are usually purchased in stacks of twenty, and you can buy into the game for as little as $2 where the minimum bet is 10 cents. You can, of course, place a higher unit value on them yourself. For instance, if you paid $10 for the same stack of 20 chips they would be worth 50 cents each. The house employs small round markers with the numbers 5, 10, 20, 25, 50, 100, 500, or 1,000 to denote what a stack of twenty chips of the color the player is using is worth in dollars if the stack is valued at more than the minimum. Stack values for any intermediate amount can be designated by employing two or more markers to reach that figure. Chip color has no money value and casinos usually carry about six to eight different colors of chips and 200 or 300 of each color at a layout. The reason for the different colors is quite obvious. The croupier, or dealer, knows which player made what bet. If, on the other hand, all the chips on the table were the same color and if a number was hit, he would not know whom to pay. To avoid any arguments each player has a different color chip and everyone at the table knows to whom they belong.

Let us see how these markers determine the value of your color of chips. Suppose Lady Luck is on your side, you may find yourself in possession of the majority of the chips of the color you are playing with. When this occurs, the croupier will suggest that you have your chips revalued. In other words, he requests that you turn in some chips and he will make the ones that you still have on hand worth more. Let us say, for example, that you purchased fifty chips for $5, worth 10 cents each, and won $20 worth in your playing, so you have now 250 chips and the house has but fifty of the same color left. The easiest way for the house to replenish its supply is for the croupier to take back 200 of your chips. Then he places a $10 marker on the stack of fifty chips you have in your possession. These chips, of course, are now worth $10 a stack, or 50 cents apiece. You can, of course, refuse to have your chips revalued. The croupier will then bring in more chips of your color from one of the other layouts, or he can assign you another color if not used by the other players at your table. If you decide to stop playing, you must cash your chips in at the wheel you are playing at. Often players will take the colored chips with them when leaving the table and will try to cash them at some other casino or at some other game in the same casino they are playing and find out the hard way that they are not worth anything except at the Roulette layout. In this game, of course, the house banks all the action.

Playing the Game

Play is started by the players making their bets by placing chips on the spaces of the layout as prescribed by the rules of the game. As the bets are being made the croupier, or dealer, starts the wheelhead spinning in a counter-clockwise direction, tosses the Roulette ball on the bowl's circular back track so that it moves clockwise. While the wheel and ball are in motion, bets may be placed until the moment the croupier calls: "No more bets!" He does this when the ball appears to slow down and is about to drop off the circular track. Bets placed on the layout after his announcement are *not* valid and are returned to the player or players immediately.

When the ball drops in a canoe or pocket, the croupier immediately declares the winning number and its color, and he points with his index finger to the corresponding number on the layout. He then collects all losing bets, making sure not to touch the chips resting on winning spaces. Finally, the winners are paid off with the correct amount of chips due each winning bet. The signs 0 and 00 win for the house all bets except those placed on zero and double zero.

A standard Roulette table with its single layout is usually operated by two croupiers, while a double-end table, because of its two layouts, is worked by either three or four croupiers. The croupier who spins the wheel and deals the game is called the *wheel-roller* by casino employees. He is in full charge of the conduct of the game. His main duties are: selling chips to players, spinning the wheel, tossing the Roulette ball, declaring winners, collecting losing bets, and paying off winning bets. The other croupiers separate and stack the losing chips that have been collected or swept from the layout by the dealer. They stack the chips in piles of twenty of the same color and place them in the chip rack on the table's apron. They may also help the wheel-roller pay off winning bets by stacking the correct number of chips in a convenient place to the left of the table's apron. Incidentally, the croupier dealing the wheel is obliged to drop the ball with the hand nearest the wheel.

Compared to other gambling games, the pace is rather slow at Roulette. Many casinos try to establish a rhythm by which there will be a fixed number of coups, or turns, of the wheel per hour: forty-five to fifty-five. Playing four hours a day, the subsistence gambler gets in about 200 bets.

Roulette Bets, Odds and Percentages

The betting in Roulette is by no means restricted to a single number. As a matter of fact, most of the bets which are made are combination propositions. Without the combination (or group bets), if the player wished to bet on all the black squares, for instance, he would have to put eighteen separate bets on the table. But with the various combination bets available, a player may place a single bet which, depending on the combination selected, will cover from two to eighteen squares at a time. For the different combinations the player places his chips down on the layout in a variety of different ways. For the beginner the betting placements, or rules, can be quite confusing, so let us review all the bets which can be made along with the odds they pay and the house advantage or percentage.

Straight or Single-Number Bet. Place your chips squarely on one number on the layout, making certain that the chips do not touch any of the lines enclosing the number. This indicates that you are betting the number to win.

Payoff odds: 35 to 1.

True odds: 37 to 1. (There are 36 numbers on the wheel plus the signs 0 and 00, making a total of 38.)

Percentage favoring the house: 5.27 per cent.

The Signs 0 and 00: These can be played the same as any straight or single-number bet. The house's favorable advantage is the same as on a straight bet: 5.27 per cent.

Split or Two-Number Bet. You place your chips directly on any line separating any two numbers. If the winning number is one of the two wagered on, you win.

Payoff odds: 17 to 1.

True odds: 18 to 1.

Percentage favoring the house: 5.27 per cent.

Street or Three-Number Bet. Placing your chip or chips on the outside line of the layout indicates that you are betting on the three numbers opposite the chips, going across the layout. If the winning number is one of these three, you win.

Payoff odds: 11 to 1.

True odds: 11⅔ to 1.

Percentage favoring the house: 5.27 per cent.

Note: A three-number bet can also be made on 0, 00 and 2 by placing your wager on the intersection of the three spaces. If the winning number is one of these three, you will win at the payoff odds of 11 to 1.

Square, Quarter, Corner or Four-Number Bet. You place your chips on the intersection of the lines between any four numbers. If any one of these four numbers wins you collect.

Payoff odds: 8 to 1.

True odds: 8½ to 1.

Percentage favoring the house: 5.27 per cent.

Line, House or Five-Number Bet. Place your chips on the line separating the 1, 2, 3 from the 0 and 00 spaces at a corner intersection. This indicates that you are betting that one of the numbers 1, 2, 3, 0 or 00 will win.

Payoff odds: 6 to 1.

True odds 6⅗ to 1.

Percentage favoring the house: 7.9 per cent.

Note: The house percentage for Roulette is the same for all wagers except for the five-number bet. This bet cannot be paid at the same odds as all the other wagers because five will not divide into 36 evenly like all other bets. Consequently the house takes the advantage. This is why this wager is so often called the "house bet." From the player's standpoint, however, it is a bet that should be avoided.

Line or Six-Number Bet. Place your chip or chips on the intersection of the side line and a line between two "streets." If any of these six numbers wins, you collect.

Payoff odds: 5 to 1.

True odds: 5⅓ to 1.

Percentage favoring the house: 5.27 per cent.

Column or Twelve-Number Bet. You place your chips on one of the three blank spaces at the bottom of the layout (some layouts have three squares marked 1st, 2nd, 3rd). This indicates that you are betting the twelve vertical numbers above the space wagered on.

Payoff odds: 2 to 1.

True odds: 2⅙ to 1.

Percentage favoring the house: 5.27 per cent.

Dozens or Twelve-Number Bet. You place your chips on one of the spaces of the layout marked 1st 12, 2nd 12, or 3rd 12. The 1st 12 indicates that you are betting on the numbers 1 to 12 inclusive; the 2nd 12, the numbers 13 to 24 inclusive; and the 3rd 12, the numbers 25 to 36 inclusive.

Payoff odds: 2 to 1.

True odds: 2⅙ to 1.

Percentage favoring the house: 5.27 per cent.

Low-Number Bet. By placing your chips on the layout space marked 1 to 18, you indicate that you are betting on the numbers 1 to 18 inclusive.

Payoff odds: 1 to 1 (even money).

Correct odds: 1⅑ to 1.

Percentage favoring the bank: 5.27 per cent.

High-Number Bet. By placing your chips on the layout space marked 19 to 36, you indicate that you are betting on the numbers 19 to 36.

Payoff odds: 1 to 1 (even money).

Correct odds: 1⅑ to 1.

Percentage favoring the bank: 5.27 per cent.

Red Color Bet: You place your chips on a space of the layout marked RED. (Some layouts have a large red diamond-shaped design instead of the word RED.) You are betting that the winning color will be red.

Payoff odds: 1 to 1 (even money).

True odds: 1⅑ to 1.

Percentage favoring house: 5.27 per cent.

Black Color Bet: This is the same as a red color bet except that you place your chips on the space marked BLACK, or the black diamond, and are betting that the winning color will be black.

Even-Number Bet: You place your chips on the space of the layout marked EVEN. You are betting that the winning number will be an even number.

Payoff odds: 1 to 1 (even money).

True odds: 1⅑ to 1.

Percentage favoring house: 5.27 per cent.

Odd-Number Bet: This is the same as the even-number bet, except that you place your chips on the space marked ODD, and are betting that the winning number will be odd.

Before leaving the subject of making a bet, it might be wise to say a word about the size of wager permitted. While the maximum limits vary slightly from casino to casino, the following are fairly standard in Las Vegas:

Type of Bet	Maximum Limit	Type of Bet	Maximum Limit
Straight	$25	1st, 2nd, 3rd dozen	$250
Split	$50	Color (Red or Black)	$500
Street	$75	Even	$500
Quarter or Corner	$100	Odd	$500
House	$100	1 to 18 (Low)	$500
Line	$100	19 to 36 (High)	$500
Columns	$250		

While the maximum limit on a straight bet appears small—at various times a few casinos have raised the ceiling to $50 or $75—you must remember that the payoff for a single number wager at a $25 limit is $875. In addition, a single number may also be played with $25 straight and another $25 placed on split, corner, street, line or other bets. In other words, a maximum of $25 can also be bet any way you can reach the number.

Most casinos in Vegas also have minimum bets. As was previously mentioned, when you take your place at the Roulette table, you inform the croupier what value you desire on your chips. If you place a low denomination—10 cents or 25 cents—on them, the house may require you to wager a minimum number of chips on each spin of the wheel. This minimum is generally either three or four chips, solely at the discretion of the casino. But this does not mean that all the chips required to conform to house minimums must be placed on one particular bet. You can put one chip on a single-number wager, another on a split or street, and a third on either a corner or line. However, you cannot place them on 2–1 or even-money bets. On any one of these, you would have to wager all three or four chips on one spot. Since betting limits vary from casino to casino, it is a good idea to check with the croupier before starting your play. Remember that betting at Roulette is not a mystic art taught to or learned by only a select group. Knowing where to place your bet and what to wager provides you with the same advantage as the other players at the table.

American versus European Roulette

One problem many visitors to Las Vegas have, especially if they have played Roulette in Europe, is the difference in the house's advantage. While most gambling games are more or less universal in their play, odds and percentages, Roulette is the exception. In European Roulette, the house's advantage is considerably less because it has only zero on its layout. Also many European casinos use an *en prison* rule. That is, on even money bets, such as Odd-Even and Red-Black, this rule provides that the appearance of the zero does not result in a loss. The bet is placed *en prison*, and the outcome is determined by the next spin of the wheel. The appearance of an odd number would free all odd wagers, but without any additional payoff, while even bets would be collected by the house in the normal fashion. In a similar manner, an even designation would release even bets, and the wagers on odd would be collected. The same procedure is followed for the other even money bets. If the player desires, he can remove half of his bet, with the other half collected by the house. In American casinos, of course, all even money wagers are lost on the appearance of the zero or double zero. On a European layout that permits the *en prison* rule, the house advantage is 1.37 per cent. This can be compared to a low of 5.27 per cent in the American double zero game. For the single zero game without the *en prison* feature, the favorable percentage is 2.71 per cent. In the few European layouts that have no zero, the house advantage is 2.50 per cent. Here is a complete comparison between American and European Roulette:

American Name	French Name	Payoff	American Double Zero House %	One Zero House %	European One Zero en prison House %
Red & Black	Rouge et Noir	1 to 1	5.27	2.71	1.37
High & Low	Passe et Manque	1 to 1	5.27	2.71	1.37
Odd & Even	Impair et Pair	1 to 1	5.27	2.71	1.37
Dozens or Column	Douzaine ou Colonne	2 to 1	5.27	2.71	1.37
6 Numbers (Line)	Sixain	5 to 1	5.27	2.71	1.37
5 Numbers (House) *		6 to 1	7.90		
4 Numbers (Square)	Carre	8 to 1	5.27	2.71	1.37
3 Numbers (Street)	Transversale	11 to 1	5.27	2.71	1.37
2 Numbers (Split)	Cheval	17 to 1	5.27	2.71	1.37
1 Number (Straight)	Enpleine	35 to 1	5.27	2.71	1.37

* The five-number bet on 0, 00, 1, 2 and 3 can be made only on the American layout, since in Europe only one zero or no zeros are employed.

Systems

Roulette seems to attract more so-called "system players" than any other casino game. While thousands—or even millions—of systems have been developed to beat Roulette, *all* have failed. The major fallacy in most systems is that they give the little white ball a mind of its own. By this we mean that they are based on the premise that a Roulette ball is completely aware of the law of averages and that it will eventually do its best to balance whichever side of the ledger that has indicated signs of lagging behind. The trouble is that the little white ball—as well as a system maker —does not think. To the ball, each spin of the wheel is completely independent of the last one and has no bearing whatsoever on the upcoming one.

Many people arrive at Vegas each year with the "finest system" yet. They have worked long hours with slide rules, calculators— and even computers—on the way to beat Roulette. When they first arrive, many of them start to win—because Lady Luck smiled at them. But just when they think their "system" is unbeatable and start to bet heavily, Lady Luck turns her back and they lose. Instead of quitting, however, they continue to follow their system to recoup, and throw away more money. In other words, system gamblers play over such a long period of time, they inevitably lose one bankroll after another.

Lou Miller tells the story of the four Ivy League graduate students who really had *the* system. They had worked for a year—with help of all the mathematical devices of the university—on a way to beat Roulette. They were well on way to doing just that because after three nights at the Riviera and several other casinos, they had amassed winnings of over $25,000. But then, according to Lou Miller, they became over-confident and continued to play on. Their winning system reversed itself and all their winnings as well as their original investment went to the casinos. Miller ends his tale with a little bit of expert advice that we all should remember while gambling: "Press your luck when you are winning, but once things begin to go wrong—move on."

If there is one point that cannot be stressed too greatly when discussing Roulette, it is the idea of playing at a moderate pace with moderate losses in mind, with self-control as the master. The famed mathematician and gambling expert, Oswald Jacoby, best stated the chances of getting lucky in Roulette with his following findings:

On 500 bets you have in Roulette a $\frac{1}{10}$ chance of winning one chip *or more*. Of course, if you make less than 500 bets, you have a better chance of winning: for fifty bets you have 1 chance in 3 of winning one or more chips; if you make 100 bets your chances of winning one or more chips drops to about 1 in 4; for 200 bets, the odds are 1 in 5.

Without a doubt these are gloomy calculations, and we will not quarrel with them. They stand as fair warning to anyone who intends to play the game for any great length of time, because he will certainly lose. But, if you play for small stakes and do not take the game too seriously, Roulette is a fine way to spend a few leisurely hours. But, it is no game to try to "break the bank at Las Vegas."

6

Games of Cards—Poker, Pan, Baccarat and Faro

"It's not whether you win or lose, it's how you play the game," may be said for the world of sports, but it has no place in the gambling world, where the most important thing is to win. As for games of cards, the saying should be paraphrased; "Whether you win or lose depends on how you play the game."

In many of Las Vegas' casinos, there are card rooms where you can play Poker and Pan in a comfortable and congenial atmosphere. In these rooms, the casinos either take a fixed percentage—usually 5 per cent—out of the pot or level a tax or charge against each player on each hand. This is reasonable enough, and it pays the casino's overhead and earns the operation a profit. Since both Poker and Pan get fairly good play it is sometimes quite a lot of profit. But, for this fee, the house furnishes the dealer—which is a *most* important point for the "amateur" card-player.

It is a good general rule, especially in Poker, to play *only* in a casino game. At any other location in Las Vegas the average poker-player could be cheated blind by a card sharper. But at a casino, the dealer, who is a professional, keeps the game as honest as possible. You might notice, in a casino game, how closely the dealer will watch the hands of an obvious "smoothy," someone he has spotted as a possible cheater. This fellow usually has super-sharpened fingernails. He will either make a slight scratch on all Aces and big cards as he can in, say, three or four rounds of the cards, or he will use some other identifying mark. The dealer may spot this right off the deal, and when this player tosses a $5 chip out there instead of the $1 one that he has been betting, the dealer will pull the cards and start with a fresh deck. When the pit boss comes by, the dealer will hand him the deck, and nod at the man in question. If the man has been up to some monkey business, he will be barred from the casino for life. Remember that in both Poker and Pan you play against fellow players, *not* the house.

Poker

Poker has become the national card game of the United States because it so well suits the American temperament. It is a game for the individual. In it, the player is on his own, the master of his own fate. There are, of course, other reasons why Poker is such a timeless favorite.

While it is often called the American national game—sharing this distinction with baseball—it is popular throughout the world. While the history of Poker is rather difficult to trace, it combines principles of card games known for centuries in Europe and probably long before that in the Orient, but in its present form it is distinctly of American origin. While no one can prove it, most poker historians believe that our name Poker was derived from the French game of *poque*. This card game was first introduced to our country from France in the early 1800's along the Mississippi River and in New Orleans. It spread throughout the south and southern gentlemen from the cotton plantations—untutored in French pronunciation—decreed that according to its spelling the name should have two syllables. So they changed "poque" to "po-que," or "po-kuh." Later it is believed that the southern pronunciation of the game po-kuh was given a northern touch, and hence Poker.

There is a popular misconception that Poker is just a game of pure luck. Actually, nothing could be further from the truth. Poker is a game of skill, with luck playing only a very minor role in the outcome of any game. Sure you can have a run of bad cards, but the way you play through it is very much the measure of your skill. In other words, if you are losing consistently, you're not unlucky. You're just being outplayed.

Despite the fact that there are innumerable forms of Poker and that the strategy differs slightly in all of them, good players will almost always wind up winners and poor players will almost always wind up losers. But to become a good Poker player, you must learn the art—and it is an art—and skill of Poker. Fortunately, however, the art and skill of Poker is not a matter of years of practice. It has often been stated that to become a first-rate Poker player, you must be one part mathematician, one part economist, and one part psychiatrist. While this is undoubtedly true, as these skills apply to Poker, they can be learned. Not overnight, to be sure, but much more quickly than you might expect. It would be, of course, foolish for a beginner in Poker to sit in on a Las Vegas game. Get your practice in friendly games first.

There are three basic types of Poker—Draw, Stud and Lo-Ball—played in Vegas' casinos. Let's take a look at the strategy of each.

Draw Poker

In this game, five cards are dealt, one at a time in rotation, face down, to each player. There is then a betting interval, after which each active player in turn may discard one or more cards and the dealer serves him that number of cards from the top of the pack, to restore his hand to five cards. (A player need not draw; he may play the cards originally dealt to him, in which case he is said to "stand pat.") After the draw, there is another betting interval, followed by a showdown. The best or highest-ranking hand, of course, wins the pot.

THE POKER HANDS. A poker hand consists of *only* five cards. The value of a hand depends on whether it contains one of the following combinations:

Straight flush, the highest possible hand: all five cards of the same suit and in sequence, as the 5, 6, 7, 8, and 9 of diamonds. The highest-ranking straight flush is the A, K, Q, J and 10 of one suit, called a *royal flush.*

Four of a kind rank next under a straight flush; as four Aces or four 7s. It doesn't matter what the fifth, unmatched card is.

A *full house* is three cards of one rank and two cards of another rank, 9-9-9-3-3, and ranks next under four of a kind.

A *flush* is five cards of the same suit, but not all in sequence, and ranks next below a full house.

A *straight* is five cards in sequence, but not all of the same suit.

It loses to a flush or higher hand, but beats anything else.

Three of a kind rank next under a straight.

Two pair, as K–K–6–6–3, rank next under three of a kind.

One pair beats any hand containing no pair but none of the higher-ranking combinations above.

And below the rank of hands containing one pair are all the no-pair hands, which are rated by the highest card they contain, so that an Ace-high hand will beat a King-high hand, and so on.

Since the most popular form of Draw Poker by far in casinos is that of jackpots (Jacks or better), we will stress the strategy of this game. However, most of the points will apply to every form of Draw Poker.

WHEN TO OPEN. To open the first round of betting in jackpots, as previously stated, a player must have a pair of Jacks or better. The privilege of opening goes to the first player to the left of the dealer and, if he passes, to the next player on the left, and so on until the pot is opened or the deal is passed around and a new one started. But, even if you have openers you have the option of betting or passing. In other words, there are times, depending upon your position (closeness to the dealer) and the number of players in the game, when it may be unwise, even though you have the necessary requirements, to be the first to open.

Most experts agree that in a game with five players or less, you should open the pot even if you just have a pair of Jacks. If you are under the gun (next to the dealer) with six in the game you should pass a pair of Jacks or Queens. In the other positions open with any legal openers. If seven or eight are in the game, the player under the gun shouldn't open on less than Aces; the second and third men should open only on Kings or better; fourth and fifth on Queens; after that on Jacks. Two pairs, however low, are always adequate to open any position. The reason behind the logic of these simple rules is based on the fact that with only four to hear from the chances are that no one will raise you since the probability of better hands is less and there is a chance that a player or two will drop. With more players in the game the chances of winning on a pair of Jacks becomes increasingly poorer and the chances that someone after you will raise your opening bet are very good. If you pass your minimum openers and someone else opens the play, you can stick around to draw to your holding generally with a minimum bet. If someone does not open, there's always another hand, and you must be satisfied to know that you played the hand the way the experts would.

CHANCE OF BEING HIGH IN THE FIRST FIVE CARDS

	Number of Opponents						
Your Hand	1	2	3	4	5	6	7
Three of a Kind	.97	.94	.92	.89	.87	.84	.82
Two Pair	.93	.86	.80	.74	.68	.63	.59
Pair of Aces	.89	.79	.70	.62	.55	.49	.43
Pair of Kings	.88	.78	.69	.61	.54	.48	.42
Pair of Queens	.83	.68	.56	.46	.38	.32	.26
Pair of Jacks	.79	.63	.50	.40	.32	.25	.20

To further validate this strategy, the chart here shows that the chances of being high in the first five cards decreases as the number of players increases: i.e., with three other players in the game the chances of being high with Jacks is 50 per cent, or 2 to 1 odds; with six opponents to worry about the odds raise to 4 to 1 while the percentage decreases to 25. Therefore, in the latter case you need a better hand to win and should not always open on an absolute minimum. There is an old Poker adage that states: High man going into the draw has the best chance of winning the pot. In other words, if, before the opening bet, you are sitting with better cards than your opponents', the odds favor your winning the hand—provided, of course, you stay until the final bet. By using the table just mentioned above and the table below which lists how often you can expect any combination of cards to show up in the first cards dealt, you can get a pretty good idea how your hand rates with opponents' going in.

Ranking order of Hands	*Chances of Being Dealt in the Original Five Cards*	*Number of Possible Ways Hand Can Be Made*
Royal Flush	1 in 649,740	4
Straight Flush	1 in 64,974	36
Four of a Kind	1 in 4,165	624
Full House	1 in 694	3,744
Flush	1 in 509	5,108
Straight	1 in 255	10,200
Three of a Kind	1 in 47	54,912
Two Pairs	1 in 21	123,552
One Pair	1 in 2½	1,098,240
No Pair	1 in 2	1,302,540

Sometimes it is even wise strategy, especially when there are more than five other players, to pass a good hand—three of a kind —under the gun. When someone else opens, you can call and not take over the driver's seat (position of advantage) until after the draw.

POSSIBLE HANDS OF LESS VALUE THAN ONE PAIR

Ace High	502,860
King High	335,580
Queen High	213,180
Jack High	127,500
Ten High	70,380
Nine High	34,680
Eight High	14,280
Seven High	4,080
Total	1,302,540

Staying in. Whether you stay in a hand depends on the cards originally dealt and your chances of improvement through the draw. To help you make your mind on the latter point, the table here should be carefully studied. It reveals the odds against improving any given hand in draw poker, when the rule is "Jacks or better" to open the pot.

As you can see from the chart on page 99, you are best off with a maximum draw: that is, three cards when you have a pair, or two cards when you have three of a kind.

In jackpots it usually is considered very poor Poker strategy to stay in with less than a pair of Jacks and most good players even fold on them, believing that Queens or better are minimum to stay with. To save two unmatched cards and draw a small pair will do absolutely no good. Even if you hold a small pair and catch a second pair—only once in every five draws—you stand a good chance of losing because the odds are all with the players with the better hands. Of course, if you insist on fattening up the pot by playing poor cards, you must expect to lose. The only possible exception to this is when the ante is big due to repeated passes on previous hands. But, even in such cases, do not stay unless the odds the pot is offering are as good or better than the odds of your winning the pot if your draw is successful.

To figure the odds that the pot is offering, or, as it is generally

Cards held in hand	Cards drawn		Odds against making
One pair	3	Two pair	5 to 1
		Three of a kind	8 to 1
		Full house	97 to 1
		Four of a kind	359 to 1
		Any improvement	2½ to 1
One pair with Ace kicker	2	Aces up	7½ to 1
		Another pair	17 to 1
		Three of a kind	12 to 1
		Full House	119 to 1
		Four of a kind	1,080 to 1
		Any improvement	3 to 1
Two pairs	1	Full house	11 to 1
		Any improvement	11 to 1
Three of a kind	2	Full house	15½ to 1
		Four of a kind	22½ to 1
		Any improvement	8½ to 1
Three of a kind and one odd card	2	Full house	14½ to 1
		Four of a kind	46 to 1
		Any improvement	11 to 1
Four-straight, open ends	1	Straight	5 to 1
Four-straight, one end or inside	1	Straight	11 to 1
Four-flush	1	Flush	4½ to 1
Four-straight flush, both ends open	1	Straight flush	22½ to 1
		Any improvement	2 to 1
Four-straight flush, one end or inside	1	Straight flush	46 to 1
		Any improvement	3 to 1
One Ace	4	Pair of Aces	3 to 1
		Aces up	14 to 1

called the *pot odds*, you simply count (roughly) the number of chips in the pot. If, for example, the ante in a six-handed game is one chip, and the two men before you—one opens for two and the other calls for two—have put in four chips, there should be ten chips in the pot when it comes your turn to call. Since you must pay two chips to stay, the pot offers you 5 to 1 odds. Now you should compare the odds against your chances of winning the pot; suppose you have a four-card flush, in which case the odds are 38 to 9, or somewhat more than 4 to 1, that you would not make a flush on a one-card draw. Since the pot offers you 5 to 1, and the odds against your making the flush are only 4 to 1, you should put in the two chips and play. Such calculation is worthless, of course, unless you are virtually sure of winning the pot if your draw is successful. If there is any appreciable danger that you may make the flush and still lose, you should not play. For instance, you should fold in such a pot if it has been raised more than once. The old adage about throwing good money after bad is definitely applicable here. Remember that by checking your chances from the improvement chart (page 99) plus judging your opponents' possible strength, you will be able to determine whether to stay or not.

WHEN TO RAISE. To raise the pot after the betting has been opened is generally done for two reasons: (1) to drive other players out of hand; and (2) to increase the size of the pot. Generally speaking, it is not the best strategy to drive other players out when you think that you have the best hand since poker probabilities show that the best hand going in is a consistent winner. Therefore if you have three of a kind (10s or better) or a pat hand, you should never raise; you should just call, hoping to lure in other players and increase the size of the pot before your good hand is revealed.

In some cases, however, a raise before the draw to drive players out is good strategy. For example, if you have two pair in a seven-hand game, there is a 63 per cent probability (see page 97) that your hand is high before the draw; but the odds are 11 to 1 that you would not improve it. It is standard practice to raise the opener on such a hand, to drive out the other players before they can draw, improve their hands, and perhaps best you. This is especially true in a game in which players make a general habit of staying in with any type of pair, straight, or flush draw. Eliminate as much competition as quickly as possible in such cases.

The exception to this strategy is if you have a high two pairs, such as Aces or Kings up. In this case you do not want to eliminate your competition since you have a good chance of winning even against players who stay and improve, but who get no better than Queens up. As a general rule, however, if you hold a weak two pairs (Jacks up or lower), raise immediately to drive out any players who want to ride along on a cheap hand and also to see if your opponents have better hands than yours. Since a raise has been made, the really good hand—three of a kind and better—will reraise at this point since most of the undecided players will have dropped on the first raise.

When betting or raising it is well to keep in mind that you must conceal your purposes and intentions as best you can. To do this, you must vary betting and raising techniques so as to keep your opponents guessing. It is not necessary to play unsoundly in order to vary your game; there are often several sound methods of playing any particular hand in any given situation. For example, you should sometimes raise before the draw on a good hand; such as three of a kind or better; at other times you should wait, draw one card as though to a straight or flush possibility and then bet after the draw. You should sometimes open the pot on a good hand, and at other times wait until someone else has opened and then raise.

Position play is very important in Poker and occasionally by raising a bet in the opening interval you can create a good position for yourself from one which is naturally bad. For instance, suppose there are two other active players, whom we will call A and B, besides yourself. Player A has opened and Player B has raised. While you have a good hand, very likely the best, you are afraid of both opponents and you can foresee a possible situation after the draw in which A will check to the raiser, B will bet, and you will be caught in a bad position between the two of them. (In casino play, while the dealer remains the same, his position theoretically shifts one player after each deal.)

To rectify your bad position, it may be wise to reraise rather than call since normally A and B will check to you after the draw and, if your hand has not picked up any strength, you can check, too, and get a free showdown. If they check and you have improved your hand, then bet the cards for all they are worth. However, if either of the other two players bets into you after the draw, you can assume that he has improved, and you should drop. Thus making a raise or reraise at this point is most strategic because the betting is usually lower before the draw than after. By making your move here at a low level you save yourself a dangerous call at a higher or more expensive level.

MAKING THE DRAW. When making the draw, you have two purposes: 1) to improve your hand; and 2) to deceive the other players. If your main object is to just improve your hand, your best move is to make the maximum draw: that is, if you have one pair you draw three cards; is you have three of a kind to start with you draw two cards; and if you have two pairs, one card. While sometimes you will need some specific degree of improvement, it may be more important to deceive the other players than to improve your hand. In other words, in the latter case, you hold a kicker to a pair, while with three of a kind you will draw one card and with a high pair up you will stay pat. The advantage of keeping your opponents guessing by varying your play offsets, as just discussed, the lessened chance of improvement. Remember that a winning Poker player is one who occasionally varies his draw.

Many good Poker players, when they have three of a kind, draw just one card, since their chances of winning without improvement are good. When you hold a kicker, you do not represent your hand too strongly before the draw and players with two pairs are likely to at least call you, since a one-card draw usually indicates two pairs, especially when you open.

TWO-CARD DRAW. When you make a two-card draw it advertises to your opponents that you have three of a kind or are holding a pair with an Ace kicker. (Drawing two cards to a plain three-card flush or three-card straight is unsound Poker.) When you hold three of a kind, especially if you have less than four opponents, the odds are all in your favor that you will have the winning hand at the showdown even if you do not improve it. Therefore, while a two-card draw gives you a much better chance to make four of a kind and slightly better chance to show any sort of improvement, in most hands it would not make too much difference if you drew two cards, one card, or even stood pat; you would still win. For this reason, the draw to three of a kind is usually just a matter of personal tactics.

When you keep an Ace kicker with your pair and draw only two instead of three, you reduce your chances of improvement slightly, but such a move does have other compensations—if you want them. For instance, a high pair with an Ace or King kicker is a good combination to hold as a bluff on the chance you do make two pairs and no better. (With a kicker your chances of making two pairs are slightly better than with a three-card draw. Against this, your chances of getting three of a kind dwindles from 1 out of 8 to 1 out of 12.) But you should not use this strategy too often, or you will become tagged and the bluff value will be lost.

THREE-CARD DRAW. A pair is the only logical three-card draw. In some cases, especially when there are only three or four other players, you might draw three cards to an Ace-King of the same suit, and hope for the best. However, all too often you will come out with just what you went in with, a no pair hand with Ace high. If you make a pair of Aces or a pair of Kings, you may beat a player who opened on Jacks or Queens, but never forget that he may have bettered his hand, too. In actual practice, it is usually foolish to draw two unmatched cards, unless the pot odds are very good.

SPLITTING OPENERS. It is permissible to split openers and the face need not be announced. (In some instances, house rules require that a player announce that he is splitting openers and the discard is kept beside him.) For example, let's suppose you open the pot holding DQ, SQ, SJ, S10, S9. With this hand, you wish to take the chance of drawing to the possible straight flush of SQ, SJ, S10, S9. You may then discard the DQ and draw one card. It's generally considered good Poker to split openers to draw to a straight flush, but it's unwise to do it to draw to an ordinary straight or flush. The discards of the opening player should go in the pot, together with the chips, so that the openers may always be demonstrated.

Watching your discards. By studying your discards, you may get some ides how good your hand is or will be. For instance, suppose you were dealt a hand containing Q, Q, A, K, 7. Under most conditions your discard would be the A, K, 7. If you caught another Queen in draw, you could bet your three ladies like they were Aces. Why? Simply because by your discarding the Ace and King the chances of one of the other players having three of them is very remote even if, by chance, he did go in with a pair of Aces or Kings. Thus by remembering your discards, it is often possible to determine to a degree the possibilities of your opponents.

BETTING AFTER THE DRAW. After the draw, you should concern yourself with the answers to these four questions:

1. How did my hand rate against my opponents going in?
2. How many cards did my opponents take in the draw?
3. Did I improve my hand in the draw?
4. Am I playing against conservative or wild players?

The answer to the first question is often answerable by the second. By knowing your opponents' betting patterns before the draw and by knowing the number of cards they took, you should be able to judge approximately the type of hand they are holding and be able to rate yours against theirs. The answer to number three is quite obvious. But, if you have improved your hand to the point where the odds indicate that you will be high man at the showdown, be sure to make your opponents pay through the nose to see what you have got. In such cases, remember the old saying, "Charity begins at home," and play your hand accordingly.

To be successful in betting, you should study and know the habits of the other players in the game. Then, when you think you may have the winning hand, remember how they played their current hands and what type of hands they usually play that way. It is impossible to tell, of course, whether or not they have improved; but you do know that the odds against improvement of any hand runs from 2½ to 1 on up. If you can be fairly certain of the sort of hands they went in with, then you may bet whenever the odds are against their having improved, provided your position is such that you would not run into one or more reraises and be doubtful as to whether you should call or drop. It should not take too long to be able to tag your opponents as either conservative or wild players. As a rule you are safer betting into the conservative player than into the wild player. Also you can make money against the conservative player by betting because you may get a call on a fair hand. On the other hand, you cannot make money against a wild player by betting since he would not generally call if he missed, and he will raise if he hit.

The purpose of the raise before the draw was to drive as many players as possible out of the game. It is unlikely that you will drive out anyone by betting after the draw (anyone, that is, who would not have gone out anyway), and there is no point in your betting unless you have improved your hand to the point where you can beat the probabilities of your opponents. For this reason, it is generally considered dangerous to bet into a one-card draw who can raise and win if he has made a straight or flush, and who probably would not even call if he did not; such a bet stands to lose everything and gain nothing. In other words, a bet at this time is poor Poker because the one-card draws have either busted and will drop, or have filled and will call or raise and probably win. In such a case your best move is to check.

When the opener checks, it generally indicates that he only improved his hand slightly or not at all. If there has been a one-card draw, however, he is probably checking for the reason given above. But, if there has been no one-card draw, and the opener checks, you should bet with two pairs or better unless there are several players at your left who have not been heard from. In this case, it is best to check too unless you have a powerhouse. But, if the opener and several players on your right check, then bet even your two pairs.

If the opener bets after the draw, and you call, and the player on your left raises, drop if the opener calls or reraises, but call if the opener drops. In the latter case, it is your job to keep the bettor honest. But, when calling under other circumstances, remember the old maxim that a good Poker player does not call. Either he has the winning hand and raises, or he has a losing hand and drops. This is an undue oversimplification. Nevertheless, the calling game is usually a losing game. No call should ever be made from curiosity or pique. The only standard for a call is: You should have a better hand than the hand on which the player against you might, in your estimation, have bet. If you find yourself consistently calling and losing, revise your style so that you do not call so often.

Never throw your cards or fold until your turn to bet comes. Premature folding is unfair to the other players in the game.

Stud Poker

There are two major varieties of Stud Poker—five-card stud and seven-card stud—played in Las Vegas' casinos. In Stud Poker, each player receives one or more cards face down—his *hole cards*—and his remaining cards face up. There is a betting interval after each round of face-up cards is dealt, and in seven-card stud, an additional betting interval after the deal of the last cards, which are dealt face down. After the betting is over, the face-down cards are exposed and the best Poker hand wins the pot.

Five-Card Stud Poker Strategy

To be a consistent winner at five-card Stud Poker as well as in other stud games, you must be a keen observer and have a great deal of patience. In this game, your ability to observe and remember what cards have shown and have been folded is the key to your success. If you cannot do this you would not know the chances that a particular opponent has a particular hole card. Also, you would not know your own chance of improving. In other words, when playing Stud Poker—either five- or seven-card—you have to watch everything and remember everything.

The patience involved in Stud Poker playing is of the self-discipline variety. Since most stud games require no ante, you do not have to bet unless you have the high card showing on the first round. Thus you can sit in the game for literally hours and hardly spend any money, just waiting for the good hand to come along. It requires patience to sit in a Poker game and have one poor hand after another, but the winning player must be prepared to do so. It is well to remember that the winnings usually always go to the stud players who are conservative at the start and bold when they think they have the best hands.

Probabilities in Five-Card Stud. In five-card stud you must make your decision to drop, stay or raise, not when you hold five cards, as in draw, but at the moment when the first two cards have been dealt to you. Generally in five-card stud, the average winning hand is the lowest among all forms of Poker—a pair of Kings or a pair of

Aces. Many pots are won on less (such as Ace high) and many pots require more, as the upcards will reveal; but it's a basic principle to stay only when the odds against making two Kings or better are less than the odds offered by the pot. The table here shows your chances, in percentage, of being high at the end of a five-card stud deal with nothing wild. Remember that in most stud games, even with seven or eight players starting, only two or three usually are around to the end.

CHANCES OF BEING HIGH AT THE COMPLETION OF THE DEAL

Your Hand	Number of Opponents						
	1	2	3	4	5	6	7
Three of a Kind	.97	.94	.92	.89	.87	.84	.82
Two Pair	.93	.86	.80	.74	.68	.63	.59
Pair of Aces	.89	.79	.70	.62	.55	.49	.43
Pair of Kings	.88	.78	.69	.61	.54	.48	.42
Pair of Queens	.83	.68	.56	.46	.38	.32	.26
Pair of Jacks	.79	.63	.50	.40	.32	.25	.20
Pair of Tens	.76	.58	.44				
Pair of Nines	.73	.53	.39				
Pair of Eights	.70	.49					
Pair of Sevens	.66	.43					
Pair of Sixes	.63	.40					
Pair of Fives	.60	.36					
Pair of Fours	.57	.32					
Pair of Threes	.53	.28					
Pair of Twos	.50	.25					

Too much has been written about the Stud Poker player's methods of appraising and outguessing his opponents. This is a quality that cannot be taught; one has it or he has not. However, the following six points of strategy will help you in the various phases of the five-card stud game. While these points of strategy do not guarantee that you will win, you are sure to lose if you do not follow them.

1. Stay in the game only when your hand is better than anything showing (will "beat the board"). This is not an infallible rule, of course, but it should be generally followed. Occasionally you may be higher than everyone save the bettor. In such instances it would be best to stay one more round. At the offset of this

section on Stud Poker strategy it was stated that patience was a very important factor in winning. While it may be very boring to sit in a stud game and have to fold one poor hand after another, the chances of winning are poor unless you bet only when you can beat anything showing. In all other cases, you should drop from the game.

2. Under no circumstances should you ever play against a pair showing when you have no pair or a lower pair. This is true regardless of how many cards you may have which, if paired, will best the pair showing. Actually, the number of "over" cards is of no consequence whatsoever. Should he have you beaten at this stage, he will figure that he has you beaten at the end and will take full advantage of this fact in the betting. Also be wary of an open pair showing even though you have it beaten with a higher pair employing your hole card. Always consider that he may possibly have another card of the same rank in the hole. As a rule a good Stud Poker player will attempt to cover up the strength of his hand when all the indications are that some concealed hand is better at this stage than his hand is. In such a case, therefore, your move will depend upon your apraisal of the player and his style, as well as the cards thus far exposed.

3. There is a time-honored Stud Poker adage that says, "Never bet into a possible cinch or 'immortal' hand (a hand which cannot be beaten, regardless of your hole card) when the player with the possible cinch can raise back." Suppose, for example, that your opponent has a pair of eights on the board showing and checks. You have a King showing and a King in the hole (called a pair "back to back," or "wired"). According to the adage you should not bet, since if your opponent's hole card makes three of a kind or two pairs for him, he can raise without fear because you cannot possibly beat him. While it is true that you cannot get into much trouble playing so cautiously as the adage suggests, it is no less true that you will lose a lot of good calls. In other words, this adage should not be too strictly construed because a stud player who never bets into a possible cinch hand will usually lose just as surely as one who always bets when he can beat the board. You must appraise each situation separately, and if on the previous betting and cards exposed you judge that your opponent's showing

cards are the best he can muster, then it is a good idea to bet if you can beat the board. This is especially true when your opponent is showing a four-card flush or straight since the odds are all against his making such a hand.

4. Taking the lead in Stud Poker is accomplished by making the first bet in any given round; or raising another player's bet. If you believe you have the best hand, it is wise to permit another player, if possible, to take the lead. If there is any danger that all the other players will check, then you must bet, it being your only opportunity to build up a good pot. If another player takes the lead and continues to bet each round, it is best to wait until the last round to bump him. By that time you may know for sure if you can definitely win. But if you are high with an open pair, on any round except the last, bet the limit. In the last, check to see where the strength lies. The situation which must be guarded against most carefully is one in which your opponent will be able to best you if his hole card has any value, and you will be too weak even to call if his hole card has no value. In such cases it is foolish to bet your open pair at any time.

5. As previously stated, it is very important for you to watch your opponents' cards most carefully, to know what cards remain in the pack. An Ace, for example, cannot be considered a good hole card if all three of the other Aces, or even two of them, have been exposed.

6. Always conceal your hole card by varying your method of play. For example, you should sometimes raise immediately with a pair back-to-back, and at other times wait until a later round. Also you should sometimes check or call when you have a cinch hand and at other times bet immediately on it. As you gain experience in the game, you will devise further methods of varying your style. Remember that it is just as important in Stud Poker to vary your style as it is in draw. Also guard against any mannerism which may conceal your hole card. Such a little habit as constantly looking at your hole card may suggest to a shrewd player that it is low since you will generally remember a really valuable card and will avoid looking again for fear that another player may catch a glimpse of it. On the other hand, a habit such as stacking chips on top of the hole card may indicate that you have a pair wired.

Seven-Card Stud Poker Strategy

In a sense, seven-card stud can be considered as a cross between five-card stud and Draw Poker. It has the basis of stud but with the element of the draw in that the players get the benefit of extra cards. But, in Draw Poker you receive five cards at the beginning of the game and may draw as many as three more cards after the first betting interval for a total of eight to work out a good hand. However, remember that you cannot reuse your discards, thus you end up the draw still playing only with five cards. In five-card stud you receive five cards and must play them as they are. But in seven-card stud, you have the unique situation of being able to manipulate a total of seven cards all at one time to fill out any five-card combination.

This unique situation of the two extra cards makes seven-card stud a very high-value game amont the Pokers. Figuring percentages in the seven-card game is usually tough for the five-card player. In the seven-card game the average winning hand is a fair three of a kind, such as three eights or above. Furthermore, because the player has seven cards to play around with, straights, flushes, and even full houses are fairly frequent. It is quite possible, after the seventh card has been dealt, for a player to hold a full house without so much as a single pair showing on board, or a straight with up-cards that appear to opposing players as being so far apart that any connection would be seemingly impossible. In other words, seven-card stud is a game of seduction and deception.

Despite the intricate phases of the game, seven-card stud's proper play is comparatively simple and you do not need to resort to close calculations and straight rules of play required in draw and five-card stud. Seven-card stud is generally the most exciting form of the game and thus is most popular in social Poker circles. It is also a game in which you can lose your money rather fast, however, especially if you disregard the basic strategy of play. Let us take a look at some points to remember.

1. The general tactics of betting and raising in seven-card stud are almost identical to those of five-card stud. The only major difference is that it's rather difficult to be sure that you ever have a

cinch hand since with three cards down at the end of the deal the unexposed combinations are almost limitless. The early bets and raises follow pretty well the same general pattern in both forms of Poker. But, at the last card, betting and raising is somewhat a more risky proposition in seven-card stud. Bluffing and other skullduggery is much less effective on the last card because it is rather difficult to know when a player may have a legitimate call, regardless of what he has shown or represented in the past rounds.

2. One of the main hazards in seven-card stud is thinking of the hand ranks as though they were in a five-card or draw game, basing the estimate on what will win on values that apply only to the games with fewer cards. You also must guard against overoptimism and stubbornness to follow the basic Poker percentages. It should be remembered that very few hands are won in seven-card stud without improvement as the game progresses. The possible exception to this is if you have a high three of a kind in the first three cards. In such cases, of course, it is quite possible to win without improvement. The winning player in this game is one who stays at the start if he has made a good draw but folds quickly if he has failed to improve by at least the fifth card. To stay with a pair, even Aces, against several other players is poor policy. Hands in seven-card stud usually range so high that one of the other players almost certainly has a superior hand. But, even in this game, it is wise to remember the old Draw Poker adage that the best hand going figures to be the best hand at the showdown. While it does not happen with the same regularity as in Draw Poker, it pays to remember the old adage when playing stud.

3. While your chances of improvement are the same, it is decidedly more advantageous to have both cards of the pair concealed than to have a split pair (one in the hole, the other face-up). For instance, suppose you have a Queen face-up and have a pair of 8s in the hole. If you draw another 8 you have three 8s, and no one is likely to suspect it. On the other hand, if you start with an 8 up and an 8 and Queen in the hole and catch another 8, you will have a pair showing and the other players are automatically on guard. If the case card (the last card) of that rank does not appear, your opponents must keep in mind the possibility that you have four of a kind, and while this may

occasionally be useful if you wish to attempt a bluff, it is far less important than the fact that it will prevent you from getting any real betting action.

4. As in five-card stud, it is very important in the seven-card variety to watch all of the cards that fall and to remember the cards that are folded during the play. This knowledge, plus the betting patterns of your opponents, is the key to the index of strength of their hands. Remember that often a simple observation can lead you to some very valuable conclusions.

Lo-Ball Poker

The following are the special rules that differentiate Lo-Ball Poker from regular Draw Poker:

Rank of Cards. The Ace is always low. A pair of Aces ranks lower than a pair of deuces.

Rank of Hands. Straights and flushes do *not* count. The lowest hand, therefore, is 5–4–3–2–A, called a *bicycle*, or *wheel*.

POSSIBLE LOW HANDS, WITH ACE LOW

King High	502,860
Queen High	335,580
Jack High	213,180
10 High	127,500
9 High	70,380
8 High	34,680
7 High	14,280
6 High	4,080
Total	1,302,540

First Betting Interval. The dealer and one or two players to his left ante; the sum of their antes equals the limit before the draw. (If the limit is 2, the dealer antes 1 and eldest hand antes 1; if the limit is 5, dealer antes 1, and the two players at his left 2 each.)

The first turn to open goes to the player to the left of the last ante. There is no minimum hand required to open. The betting before the draw is "pass and out"—each player must bet or drop. The antes count toward the amount required to call.

The Draw. A player may draw any nuber of cards, up to five.

The dealer burns a card, face down, before the draw begins. He puts this card under the chips in the pot.

Second Betting Interval. The limit is double the limit before the draw. Checking is permitted, but in some games a player who checks 7-high or better forfeits all interest in chips added to the pot after he checks. (That is, if a player checks 7-high or better, then calls a bet and loses, he loses everything; if he calls a bet and wins, the bettor against him may withdraw his bet.)

POSSIBLE LOW HANDS, ACE LOW, NO STRAIGHTS OR FLUSHES, OUT OF 2,598, 960 POSSIBLE HANDS

		Chance of Holding
10 High	129,528	1 in 20
9 High	71,904	1 in 36
8 High	35,924	1 in 72
7 High	15,384	1 in 169
6 High	5,120	1 in 508
5 High (5–4–3–2–A)	1,024	1 in 2,538
10 High or Lower	258,885	1 in 10

Skillful Play. It is seldom worthwhile to draw to anything worse than a four-card 8-high holding. The average hand after the draw is 10-high. A pat 9-high hand will win more than half the pots, and a 10-high hand will win half the pots, but it is not worthwhile to open on such a hand in an early position unless it also offers a good one-card draw to a 7–4 high or 6-high hand (in case anyone raises).

With a one-card draw to an 8, the odds are 2 to 1 against getting an 8-high hand, even money on having no worse than 10-high. With a one-card draw to a 7, the odds are 3 to 1 against getting a 7-high hand, 2 to 1 against 8-high or better, even money on having no worse than 10-high. A 7-high is even worth a bet after the draw (especially when it cannot legally be checked); a 7–5 high is worth a raise after the draw, provided no one raised before.

The Psychology of Poker

The major problem you face in any Poker game can be put succinctly as follows: Is my hand better than any of my opponents'. This problem of whether or not your hand is superior or inferior to your opponents' isn't so impossible a task as you may first suppose. An expert, indeed, will very seldom be wrong on this point. In fact, some professional players, if they make an error of this nature three or four times in a Poker session, will conclude that their judgment is so poor that evening that they had better abandon the game for the time being.

While Poker psychology—often called Poker intuition—is a rather special aptitude, it is based primarily on a very close analysis of the three basic factors of any player's make-up—habits, character, and temperament. However, the psychology of Poker will vary to such a degree that it is almost impossible to set down any specific binding rules to follow. Actually, your ability of appraising and outguessing your opponents is a special quality that cannot be taught; you either have it or you do not. But, if you have this latent talent you should develop it to the highest possible degree. If the majority of the players in the game are equal or better than you in this ability and can outguess you constantly, you simply should not play in that game.

Every one of us, in spite of our best efforts, generally have certain habits in the way we handle our cards, the manner in which we draw, the speed of making a bet, the way we stack chips on the hole cards, etc. While you should make every effort to eliminate your telltale traits, you should make every effort to use to your benefit these actions when made by your opponents. They very often might give a good clue to the strength of their hands. A long hesitation before a bet, for example, suggests a bluff, or a slow call suggests a degree of doubt. Betting high quickly or with marked deliberation, on the other hand, can be taken generally to mean a real strong hand.

As a rule, most Poker players have a definite pattern of play, or character as it is often called. By this we mean that all of us have more or less a system of standards to bet, draw, drop, raise, and even bluff. As was stated earlier, it is wise to vary one's game from time to time to prevent other players from being able to read your own game. But you should study the standards of your opponents whenever possible. The best time to do this is when you have folded early and can watch the pattern of play of your opponents who are still in the game. Look at all hands after the call and not just the winner. When a man who raised early is beaten at the showdown, see what he raised on—provided of course the hand was bet and called or checked out so that you have the right to see his holding, regardless of whether it won. It will help you form a mental picture of his character of play. In other words, character is manifested by a player's system of card values and bets.

Most Poker players fall into certain categories that are usually fairly easy to spot. The easiest way to classify your opponents is to ask yourself the following about each player in the game:

1. Does he have any give-away habits?
2. What are his betting, raising and calling standards?
3. Is he a loose or a conservative player?
4. Has he a "poker-face" or does he show his emotions easily?
5. Does he vary his game?
6. Is he a player that is noted to bluff frequently?

Properly correlated the answers will help you to develop your skill in the psychology of Poker. Remember, Las Vegas is no place to "learn" Poker. If you are not an "expert," with a *thorough* knowledge of all odds, it is wise to avoid the game. Even if you are the Friday-night Poker champ in your hometown, remember that casino Poker is the "big leagues." At just about every Poker table there is usually one person who earns his livelihood by winning from the tourist. To him, Poker is not a game of luck, but one of skill. Unless you plan to play by the odds and use Poker psychology to the utmost, do *not* take part in the game at Vegas.

Pan

Pan has suddenly become one of the most popular card games in the "Fun Capital of the World." This game, whose rightful name is *Panguingue*, is derived from *Conquian*, the father of all Rummy card games.

The fascination and excitement in playing Pan comes from the fact that it is played with eight decks of cards, from which the 8s, 9s and 10s have been removed. (Most casinos in Las Vegas also remove one full suit of spades, making a total of 310 cards in the game.) Thus, the 7 is in sequence with the Jack, and the Ace ranks low, below the deuce. Because of the number of cards in the game, they are kept in a wooden box called a "shoe."

In most casinos, an ante of one chip is required before the game starts. (Chips are valued generally at 25 cents, 50 cents, and $1—that is, there are quarter games, half-dollar games, and one-dollar games.) After the cards have been shuffled together, the permanent dealer (he is furnished by the house) takes a sufficient number from the top of the stock to deal each player ten cards, five at a time. (Preserving the tradition of Conquian, the rotation of deal and play is to the *right*, instead of to the left as in most other games.) Any cards left over after the deal are returned to the stock or dealing shoe, and the top card is then turned face up on the table beside the stock for the first player (eldest hand) to decide whether he will use it or draw the top card from the stock or shoe. The winner of the previous hand is considered the eldest hand and thus receives the first card of the deal and makes the first play. In theory, the player to the left of the previous winner is the dealer. The actual dealing, of course, is done by the house.

When the cards are dealt, each player sorts his hand into sequences and triplets (three of a kind), and determines what cards he wants to complete his runs, so that he may be on the lookout for them. The player then draws the top card from the stock and turns it face up on the pack. If this card can be used in combination with any of those in his hand, he draws it over to his side of the table, and takes from his hand the cards completing the combination of three cards, leaving them all face up. Even if he has cards enough in his hand to increase the combination to four or more cards, he should not show them. The cards drawn from the stock must *never* be taken into the hand.

Let us suppose the pone holds these cards: H J 7 6 4; C 5 3 2; D K 7 5; and that the H 5 is the first card he draws. He can use this card in three ways: By making a run of three with the H 4 and H 6; or a run with the H 6 and H 7; or a triplet with the two other 5s. In this case he would probably lay out the 6 and 7, and make the run of three. If he should draw the H Q later on, he could use it by continuing the sequence with his Jack; or if the H 3 appeared, he could use it with his H 4.

If he cannot use the card drawn, or does not wish to, he draws it from its position on the top of the stock and places it between himself and the player to his immediate right still face up. This player then decides whether or not he wants it, and if he does not he "passes" it by turning it face down, and pushing it to his right. Cards once passed in this manner cannot again be seen by either player. The player who passes the card turns up the next one on the stock. If he does not want it, he places it on the table between himself and his adversary, and if his adversary does not want it either, he turns it down and passes it to the pile of deadwood (discards), turning up the top card of the stock again. In this manner it will be seen that each player has to decide on two cards in succession; the one drawn but not used by his adversary, and the one he draws himself. This is continued until a player "goes out."

If a player uses any card drawn from the stock in this manner, it is obvious that he has too many cards, and in order to reduce his hand and show-downs to ten cards, he must discard something, unless he can show down everything remaining in his hand, in which case he would have eleven cards down, and win the game. In discarding, the card thrown out is placed at the disposal of the adversary, as if it were the card drawn from the stock, and if the adversary does not want it, he passes it and draws another. It should be observed that the player drawing the card from the stock always has the first refusal of it. This is sometimes very important, as both players often need the same card.

In the foregoing example, the player's best discard would be his D K, which is too far removed from the others in the suit to make a run possible, and there is no mate to it with which to start a triplet. If the adversary could use this King, he would have to discard in his turn, and the card so thrown out would be at the disposal of the other player, just as if it had been drawn from the stock.

A meld, as in all Rummy games, may be either a group of three cards of the same rank (such as three 4s) or a sequence of three cards in the same suit (such as D 4, 5, 6). Only three cards may be melded in the original set. But a player may add to his own melds (not to melds of other players).

The regulations in full are as follows:

Any three Aces or any three Kings, regardless of suits, form a valid set. These ranks are called *non-comoquers*. Any card of the same rank may be added to a non-comoquer set, regardless of its suit. All other ranks are *comoquers*, and a set here must be three cards of different suits or all of the same suit. To a set of cards in different suits may be added other cards of the same rank in any suit. To a set of cards all in the same suit may be added only cards that are the same in suit as well as rank. A sequence may be added to until the limit of the rank is reached, King high or Ace low.

Conditions, or pays, are certain melds for which the player immediately collects from every other active player. In the description below, *valle* (pay) *cards* refers to 3s, 5s, and 7s. The conditions are:

Three 3s, 5s, or 7s of different suits . . . . pays 1 chip.
Three 3s, 5s, or 7s of the same suit . . . . pays 2 chips.
Spades . . . . pays 4 chips.
Any other three cards in the same denomination in
the same suit . . . . pays 1 chip.
Spades . . . . pays 2 chips.
Jack, Queen, King or Ace, Deuce, Trey of the same
suit . . . . pays 1 chip.
Spades . . . . pays 2 chips.

In the course of adding cards to his melds, a player may split one meld into two, provided that each remains a valid meld, and may borrow from an amplified meld to make a new one, under the same proviso. Conditions, or pays, made by splitting or borrowing collect as though they were entirely new. Each card added to a condition collects anew for the entire condition.

The first player to meld exactly eleven cards wins the deal. Since the original hand of ten cards cannot be increased, this means that the winner at his last turn draws a card, melds it, and does not discard. A player may meld all his ten cards and have none left; in this case he continues to draw and discard until he draws a card that he can lay off. An important (an exasperating) rule is that if a discard fits with a meld of the in-turn player, he must draw it and meld it on demand of any other player. The object in making this demand is to make it more difficult for the victim to go out. If he holds two cards, which may be a pair, his chances of going out are reduced if he has to break up his pair. For instance, a player has eight cards down, two sequences of four small cards each, and in his hand a pair of Kings will make him game; but if he has to depend on his sequences to put him out, he will have to get three more cards. (Remember that the player must "go out" with 11 cards.) Suppose he draws a card that will fit one of his sequences; it is to his advantage to pass it; but upon laying it on the table any of the active players in the game at that time (players who have dropped out at beginning of the game are not considered active) may force him to take the card by placing it at the end of his sequence, at the same time saying: "Discard." The player must follow his adversary's order.

In the same manner, if the card drawn fits into a showdown sequence of his adversary to his immediate right, he or any of the active members in the game can force that player to take the card and discard one from his hand. Also a player holding one of the cards of his immediate right adversary's show-down sequence or triplet may force after using a card, by placing his discard on this adversary's sequence, instead of laying it on the table. If it is laid on the table, the adversary may, if not forced at once by an active player, turn it down, and it is then too late to compel him to use it. Suppose, for example, you think your adversary to the right holds two cards of an unplayed sequence, and has a triplet on the table. If you can use one of those sequence cards in his hand to advantage, and can force him by giving him the fourth card of his triplet, which is of no use to you, by all means do so; but you must remember that you cannot force in such a case except after using a card yourself, because you are not allowed to discard under any other circumstances.

The player who first "goes out" collects two chips from all of the active players, as well as collecting again for all the pay "spreads" in his hand. The ante is also taken by the winner. As a general rule, conditions or pay spreads are collected when the meld is made. The dealer, as in Poker, takes the house's cut of the pot, which is usually 5 per cent of the total earnings.

A player who has an incorrect hand may have it replaced with a new hand before he makes his first play; thereafter an incorrect, or foul, hand is dead but the holder must make all payments as though he were still in the game. If he has made any collections for conditions, he must return them.

An illegal meld must be made legal when attention is called to it; if the player cannot make it legal, the penalty is the same as for an incorrect hand. No play is final until a player has discarded. If a player picks up a drawn card and puts it in his hand, this move also constitutes an incorrect, or foul, hand. The dealer's decision is always final in all cases of house rules.

Pan as played at most casinos is not a "blood" game like Poker. As Rudy Lauber, who runs the Pan games at the Sahara, told us: "Pan is a game where—with average luck and knowledge—you can play for a whole night without 'getting hurt too bad.' In a quarter game, for instance, I would say $20 won or lost would be considerable money. This is true for the big games, too—$40 in a 50-cent game, $80 in a $1 one. You can have a lot of fun at Pan without costing you a lot of money."

Baccarat/Chemin de Fer

A game with a history that goes back to the Court of Charles VII in the late 15th century, Baccarat/Chemin de Fer was introduced to America in the early 1900's but its popularity was short-lived when, a year or two later, Blackjack made its debut. It was re-introduced in Vegas in 1958 and it has been increasing in popularity ever since. The game has an *average* house advantage of 1.15 per cent and is about the simplest game to play in town.

Up to twelve players can play Baccarat at one time and they sit at an oval table slotted in the center to accommodate the croupier, or dealer. The numbers that appear on the table layout represent the seat numbers of the players. Baccarat is generally played for cash—with a minimum of $5 to $20, and a maximum of $2,000. The house banks the entire game and a money-dealer collects losing wagers and pays off winners. He also keeps track of the 5 per cent commission levied on bank bets.

In Baccarat, only two hands are dealt—a player's hand and banker's hand. Strict rules determine its play so that the player does not have to make any decisions other than the size of his wager and whether to bet on the player's hand or the bank's. Bets with the player's hand are made by placing the money in front of your position in the area marked "Player." Wagers with the bank are placed in the "Banker" area in the section marked with your position number. There is no strategy that can be used to increase your chances of winning and, because it is a game of pure chance, the house advantage against bets with the player is only 1.23 per cent, and only 1.06 per cent for bets with the banker.

Baccarat is played with eight decks of cards. The cards are shuffled by the players—reshuffled by the croupier. He then inserts a blank white card six cards from the bottom of the pack. The pack is then placed in a wooden dealing shoe. The purpose of the white card is to show the croupier that only one more hand can be dealt before the cards must be reshuffled.

At the start, the bank is designated at position 1, and the player at this location deals from the shoe one card at a time face down until he has given two cards to the croupier and two cards to himself. The croupier will then hand the cards, as a matter of courtesy, to the player to the banker's right who is betting the highest amount of money against the bank (for the player). These two cards are turned over and exposed to all; at the same time the croupier calls out the player's count. Then the banker looks at his cards and turns them over for the croupier to call out the bank's total. These card totals dictate the action that follows; the player or banker has no decisions to make. The following are rules that are used in Las Vegas casinos:

RULES FOR THE PLAYER

Total of Cards Held *	*Action To Be Taken*
0–1–2–3–4–5	The Player is given an additional card.
6–7	Player must stand.
8–9	A natural—Player stands—Bank cannot draw.

RULES FOR THE BANKER

Total of Cards Held *	*Draws When Giving*	*Stands When Giving*
0–1–2	1–2–3–4–5–6–7–9–10	8
4	2–3–4–5–6–7	1–8–9–10
5	4–5–6–7	1–2–3–8–9–10
6	6–7	1–2–3–4–5–8–9–10
7	Always stands regardless of player's action.	
8–9	A natural—Banker stands—Player cannot draw.	

Note: If a player stands, the banker will draw if his hand totals 5 or lower; he will stand on 6 or higher

* Picture cards and 10s count as zero. For a total in excess of 10, the ten digit is ignored so that the count is always between 0 and 9. For example, $7 + 8 = 15 - 10 = 5$ total card count.

The object of the game is to come closest to the number 9. As we noted, picture cards and tens, and any combination of cards totaling 10, count nothing. Ace is counted one, deuce is counted two, etc. In case of a "tie," the hand is played over.

There is no need for you to memorize the rules, the croupier controls the game completely and tells the banker when to give the player or himself another card. The banker does not deal any cards except at the croupier's direction. All wagers with either the bank or with the player are, as previously stated, made against the house on an even money (1 to 1) basis. The house takes 5 per cent of winning bets made against the player. No percentage is taken of losing banker bet or bets with the player. The house advantage of 1.06 to 1.23 per cent includes the effect of this house commission; otherwise the banker would have an even greater advantage over the player. But despite the fact that that the best bet in Baccarat is to play with the bank, professional gamblers usually play both sides with equal frequency since the difference is only 1.17 per cent.

If the banker makes a "pass" and wins, he retains the shoe and deals again. When the banker loses, the shoe moves to the player on the right, thus giving each player a chance to handle the shoe, or deal. A player may pass the shoe at any time. Incidentally when you are the banker, you can bet either way—with the bank or with the player. You do not have to bet the bank. After the play of a game, the cards of both hands are placed in the discard chute.

While no private wagering is permitted, a few casinos offer side bets to the player. One of these is marked "Nine and Ten" and a bet on it means that the player is betting that the banker will make a nine on his first two cards and the payoff is at 10 for 1, or 9 to 1. Since the correct odds are approximately 9½ to 1 against this being the case, the house advantage is 5.1 per cent. A similar bet pays 9 to 1, or 10 for 1, if the total is 8, and the house percentage is approximately the same as for the bet on 9. Finally, a 4 to 1, or 5 for 1, payoff is offered if the banker's two-card total is either 8 or 9. Again, essentially the same house advantage applies. Thus, it is obvious that these side bets are best left alone.

Baccarat is a fairly fast game—about two hands a minute—and it is one of the best games for beginners; it is just as simple as slot machine play and the odds for winning are a *great* deal better. Actually, the only people who are not overly fond of Baccarat are the casino operators. Some of old-time owners are very leery of the game because the small house advantage makes it extremely difficult for the casino to recoup really big losses that can occur in this game.

Faro

Faro was once the card game of the West. Today it is *nearly* extinct, even in Las Vegas. The lack of popularity of the game is *not* due to unfavorable odds. On the contrary, a good Faro player can play the game at a very small house advantage. Actually, the lack of Faro's popularity is one of economics and difficulty of play. First, Faro is an expensive game for a casino to operate, because it requires three people—dealer, casekeeper and lookout—to run the game and only a few players can play with any degree of comfort. Also the complexity of the game requires that a player spend considerable time in learning the methods of proper betting. Thus, this section of the book is really an adventure into history rather than into contemporary gambling.

The Faro layout includes thirteen large cards representing the Ace, 2, 3, 4, 5, 6, 7, 8, 9, 10, Jack, Queen, and King of spades, although the suits have no value in the game. (It is on these cards that the players put their bets.) A standard 52-card playing deck of cards is dealt from a dealing, or Faro, box. A casekeeper, or rack, with markers representing the cards in the deck is used to case the cards as they are played. Since most players play at low house advantage, the minimum wager is usually high with encouragement to purchase a stack of chips for $25 or more to enter the game. Each player in the game has his own colored chips. For each colored chip there is a ½ chip which is placed on top of all the chips in the dealer's rack to designate the value of the player's color. Also, each color set includes a marker, a flat rectangular chip, which a player can use when his funds are too low to spread over all the cards he wishes to play. By using markers he may merely place one on each card he desires to play and if he loses the bank will deduct his losses from his chip supply. If a player wants to bet that the first card will win and the second card will lose he "coppers" his bet by placing an octagonal marker on the top of his chips. The house banks the game of Faro.

In the play of the game, each hand, or turn, the dealer deals two face-up cards from the Faro box: the first card is a losing card and the second card is the winning card. Players who have bet on the first card lose and players who have bet on the second card win an amount equal to their bet. If two like cards, that is two of a kind, appear during any turn, or deal, it is called a split and the house wins one-half the amount bet on that particular card. Suits have no value, only the rank of the cards is important. All players play against the bank only. The game is run by the *dealer* who deals the cards and acts as the bank as well as supervising all bets. The *casekeeper* keeps track of all the cards as they are dealt, while the *lookout* sits above the game and supervises the play, making certain that all bets are properly paid, and settles all disputes.

The dealer shuffles the cards and places them face up in the box. The box is provided with an open top so that the top card is clearly visible; there is a slit at the side so that the top card may be slid out of the box. The first card of the deck, which shows when the deck is first put in the box, is called *soda* and the last card is called *hock*. These two cards do not *have action*, which means that they neither win nor lose. Every other card either wins or loses.

Each player places chips on the layout so as to indicate his bet. If he places one or more chips on a card, he bets that card to win; but when coppering the bet, he is betting the card to lose. By the use of markers he may make any bet apply to two or more cards, the entire bet being determined by the first of those cards which shows. The payoff for a straight bet, and this includes a coppering bet, is 1 to 1.

When the bets have been made for the first turn, the dealer takes soda from the box and places it a few inches away from the box. He then takes the next card from the box and places it beside the box. This card loses; the card left showing in the box wins. This completes the turn, and bets on those two cards are settled. Bets may then be placed for the next turn. Bets not settled on that turn remain until the cards show up. Cards win or lose by rank only; suits have nothing to do with it.

At the next turn, the top card is placed on soda, the next losing card is placed beside the box on top of the previous losing card, and the next winning card is left showing in the box. Thus, a pile of previous winning cards is built up on soda, and a pile of losing cards is built up beside the box.

When two cards of the same order both win and lose in one turn, it is a *split*. The bank takes half of all the money bet on that card, this being the bank's only percentage.

When only three cards including hock are left for the last turn, players may bet on the exact order in which these three cards will show. (The casekeeper's record, of course, always shows which three cards they are.) The house pays 4 to 1 to any player who calls the order correctly (calls the turn).

If two of the last three cards are a pair, the house pays the proper odds of 2 to 1 for calling the turn. This is called a *cat-hop*. When three cards of one order are left, the house pays the proper odds of 2 to 1 for calling the order in which the colors of these cards will come up. A bet left on a card which can no longer show because of its order is called a sleeper and is the property of the first person who picks it up.

A player may also bet on Odd or Even; that is, that the winning (or losing) card will be odd or even, whichever the player wishes to bet. If both the winning and losing cards are odd or even the bet is a standoff. Splits are treated the same as in any other bet; the house takes one-half the bet. To bet Odd a player puts his money above the 5 (signifying odd) in line with the "High Card" line. To bet Even a player places his bet above the 2 (signifying even) in line with the "High Card" line. In addition, a player may bet that the higher of the next two cards will win by placing chips on the "High Card" or he may bet that the higher of the next two cards will lose by placing a coppered bet on the "High Card." In event of a split the bet is a standoff. A player may make as many bets as he desires on each turn.

Skillful play in Faro actually does not exist; the game is merely one of betting. The numerous systems devised for winning at the game are as futile as are all systems used in banking games. For the experienced Faro gambler, the odds for the straight bets are never more than 1.57 per cent in favor of the house and as each turn is made, the edge is substantially less—from 1 per cent to even odds.

It is not difficult to see why Faro is a fast-disappearing game in casino gambling. With a small or no advantage, how can the house afford to bank the game? Even a Faro enthusiast like Major Riddle told us: "I have refused to install a Faro game at the Dunes because the odds in favor of the house are so small that there is too much risk attached. But whenever I can find a game, I dive right in."

One-Armed Bandits— the Slot Machines

Nowhere in the casino is there the excitement of slot machine row —the flashing whirl of cherries, oranges, plums, the ringing bells, blinking lights, the tumble of coins, and the cry of "Jackpot!" all adding to the feverish activity. But in spite of all this, the simple truth is—you can't bet the slots *regularly* and win.

Actually, the "one-armed bandit," as the modern slot machine is known, is without a doubt one of the most flagrant devices ever produced to swindle the general public. From its very concept, this contrivance was geared for one purpose, that of acquiring the customer's money and at the same time providing iron-clad protection for the casino owner. That is, all slot machines are set to bring in a profit, or advantage, to the house. There is NO way to beat the slots! Yet people go on playing them frantically enough to bring in approximately 75 per cent of the downtown casinos' income. On the Strip slots account for only about 15 per cent of the income. But slots are found not only in casinos; they are in motel lobbies, taverns, clubs, lodges, bowling alleys, bus-stop restaurants, grocery stores, beauty parlors and even at airport and train station. In other words, you will find them almost any place in Las Vegas where people congregate—except churches.

Slot machines have been popular with the public ever since Charles Fey first built, in 1895, a device similar to our present day "money takers" for his San Francisco bar. This device, which he called the "Liberty Bell Slot Machine," did not pay any jackpots, only what was stated on a piece of paper pasted on the front of the machine: two horseshoes pays one drink; two horseshoes, one star, two drinks; flush of spades, four drinks; and three liberty bells, ten drinks. The machine proved popular in his bar, but Fey quickly. decided to pay off in nickels rather than drinks. Other businesses in the area requested him to make slot machines for their organizations, and soon Fey was spending all his time building "Liberty Bells."

Charles Fey's machine cost him about $20 to make. Today, a slot machine costs from $400 to $1,500. All it cost Fey in taxes was 2 cents in federal tax. This was the charge for a deck of playing cards, and a deck of cards was what he used for symbols in his early machine. He would then paste the 2 cents stamps on his slot machines. Today, between Federal, State, County or City, the taxes run better than $500 a year for each slot machine in Las Vegas. In addition, each slot machine in action earns over $4,000 a year in taxes. But this amount does not come out of the casino operators' pockets, as the slot machine pays for the taxes with the best wishes of its players, who do not seem to complain about it at all.

In Las Vegas, there are other machines, such as the automatic Blackjack machines and pinball machines, that will take your money. The latter is found only in a few of the downtown casinos and is given very little play when compared to the slots. Such machines, however, may provide a few minutes of charged relaxation at very low cost—but do not expect to win from the pinball devices.

The Slot Machine Itself

There are over 10,000 slot machines in Las Vegas—one for every eight members of the population—and they all work exactly the same, regardless of their outside appearance or the denomination of the coin—5 cents, 10 cents, 25 cents, 50 cents and $1—used. While coins are generally used with most slots, new machines have been recently introduced that will take $1 bills. It will reject $5 or any other denomination and will even reject the $1 bill if it is not inserted correctly.

Each machine contains over 500 parts and can be played twelve times a minute. Mechanically, they are beautiful pieces of machinery, precision manufactured and perfectly maintained. Every time the arm is pulled, three (sometimes four) reels are set rotating. Applied to the surface of each reel is a decalcomania of cherries, oranges, plums, bells, melons, etc. The reels spin until a retarder brings them to a stop, lining up certain combinations of picture decals. When the proper payoff combinations appear on the center line, the winnings are dropped automatically in the trough at the bottom of the machine.

PAYOFF COMBINATIONS FOR STANDARD THREE-REEL MACHINE

	1st Reel	*2nd Reel*	*3rd Reel*	*Payoff*
	Cherry	Anything	Anything	2 Coins
	Cherry	Cherry	Anything	5
	Cherry	Cherry	Cherry	10
	Orange	Orange	Bar	10
	Orange	Orange	Orange	10
	Plum	Plum	Bar	14
	Plum	Plum	Plum	14
	Bell	Bell	Bar	18
	Bell	Bell	Bell	18
Jackpot:	Melon	Melon	Bar	50
Jackpot:	Melon	Melon	Melon	50
Jackpot:	Bar	Bar	Bar	100
Double Jackpot:	7	7	7	200

The number of symbol combinations possible on the three-reel slot machines, which is the most common in Las Vegas, is 8,000. You multiply the number of symbols on the first reel by the number on the second reel ($20 \times 20 = 400$) by the number of symbols on the third reel (20) to get that 8,000 figure of possible combinations.

In the past few years, some casinos have been installing three-reel machines with twenty-five symbols. These are the machines that offer fabulous awards for small investments; i.e., a $25 or more jackpot on a three-reel nickel machine. The number of possible combinations on these machines are $25 \times 25 \times 25$, or 15,625, which is nearly double the 8,000 on the standard three-reeler.

In addition to the three reelers, a four-reel, twenty-symbol machine is being used and payoffs of $100 or more are offered for a nickel investment. The possible combinations on such a machine are (20 × 20 × 20 × 20) 160,000. Another new arrangement, with almost unbelievable jackpots, is two three-reel machines operating across the line. The number of combinations under such an arrangement is almost unbelievable—64,000,000.

There are slot machines in Las Vegas that pay off only for jackpot combinations. That is, such machines completely eliminate all drops except jackpots. Generally, they have varying amounts of jackpots. A typical machine of this type has figures of the payoff on the reels instead of fruit symbols. A nickel machine of this kind, for example, may have the figures of $2.50, $5.00, $7.50 and $10 interspersed on each of the three reels. The absence of cherries, oranges, plums, and bells, eliminates the lesser drops. If the player is successful in aligning three $7.50 in a row on the center line, for instance, he has hit the $7.50 jackpot. The frequency of jackpots on this type of machine, of course, is considerably greater than machines giving drops. This type of go-for-broke machine appeals to the go-for-broke type of player. As you see, slot machines have been designed for every type of gambling personality. For now, however, let us take a look at the complete list of the 20 symbols on each reel of a typical *standard* machine:

Space	1st Reel	2nd Reel	3rd Reel
1	Orange	Bell	Cherry
2	7	Plum & Bar	Bell
3	Bar & Bell	Plum	Melon & Orange
4	Orange	Cherry	Plum
5	Cherry	Orange	Bell
6	Bar	Bell	Cherry
7	Plum	Melon & Orange	Bell
8	Orange	Plum	Bell
9	Plum	Bell	Cherry
10	Melon	Cherry	7 & Bar
11	Plum	Bar	Bell
12	Orange	Orange	Bell
13	Plum & Cherry	Cherry	Melon & Orange
14	Bar	Bell	Plum
15	Plum	Melon & Orange	Cherry
16	Orange	Cherry	Bell
17	Melon	Bell	Orange
18	Plum	Cherry	Plum
19	Cherry	7 & Orange	Bell
20	Plum	Cherry	Plum

Note that in a few cases two symbols show in a single space, as in space 3 on Reel 1 where a Bar and a Bell are together. When this appears in the window, it counts either way—as a Bar or a Bell.

By counting the number of times each symbol appears on each reel, the following results are obtained:

	Reel 1	Reel 2	Reel 3
Cherries	2	6	4
Oranges	5	5	4 (including 1 Bar)
Plums	7	3	5 (including 1 Bar)
Bells	1	5	9 (including 1 Bar)
Melons	2	2	3 (including 1 Bar)
Bars	3	2	1
7's	1	1	1

With this information you can figure the number of payoff combinations for each symbol that can be expected to occur in the long run in each 8,000 plays.

Single-Cherry combinations: The two Cherries on Reel 1 each pay off with all the symbols on Reel 2 that are not Cherries (14), and all the symbols on Reel 3 that are not Cherries (16). Multiply $2 \times 14 \times 16 = 448$ single-Cherry combinations. Since each such combination pays two coins, there are $448 \times 2 = 896$ coins paid out.

Two-Cherry Combinations: The two Cherries on Reel 1 each pay off with the six Cherries on Reel 2 and any of the sixteen symbols on Reel 3. Multiply $2 \times 6 \times 16 = 198$ combinations, each paying five coins for a total of 990 coins.

Three-Symbol Combinations: These are all figured alike. Take Plums as an example. There are seven Plums on Reel 1, three Plums on Reel 2, and four Plums plus a Bar that counts as a Plum on Reel 3. Multiply $7 \times 3 \times 5 = 105$ combinations. Each pays fourteen coins for a total of $84 \times 14 = 1,470$ coins.

The following table shows the calculations of a standard slot machine for all symbols. Two Oranges and Bar are lumped in with three Oranges, etc.

There are, as you see when adding the last three figures in the Ways column, nineteen ways to hit a jackpot. There are a total number of 963 ways to obtain a payoff combination of some kind. Divide 963 by the total number of 8,000 plays and you find that the player can expect to get a pay-back of some type on an average of 12.4 per cent of his plays. And of the 8,000 coins put into the machine there is, in the long run, a total coin return to the player

	Symbols					
	1st Reel	2nd Reel	3rd Reel	Ways in	Payoff Coins	Total Payoff
1 Cherry	2 ×	14 ×	16 =	448 ×	2 =	896
2 Cherries	2 ×	6 ×	16 =	198 ×	5 =	990
3 Cherries	2 ×	6 ×	4 =	48 ×	10 =	480
3 Oranges	5 ×	5 ×	4 =	100 ×	10 =	1,000
3 Plums	7 ×	3 ×	5 =	105 ×	14 =	1,470
3 Bells	1 ×	5 ×	9 =	45 ×	18 =	810
3 Melons (Jackpot)	2 ×	2 ×	3 =	12 ×	50 =	600
3 Bars (Jackpot)	3 ×	2 ×	1 =	6 ×	100 =	600
3 Sevens (Double Jackpot)	1 ×	1 ×	1 =	1 ×	200 =	200
				963		7,046

of 7,046 coins. Dividing 8,000 into 7,046 gives a coin-return percentage of 88 per cent. The machine retains, over a given period, 954 of each 8,000 coins played, which is a favorable percentage for the house of 12 per cent.

The casino owners determine—for a given period, generally a week—the percentage of "take" of the various slot machines in their establishments. It is generally acknowledged by the slot machine fraternity that the ones in Las Vegas's downtown area are usually set more liberally than those in the hotels on the Strip. A survey of the major downtown casinos revealed that approximately 90 per cent of the money received by the machine is returned, with the house keeping about 10 per cent. On the Strip in hotels like Caesar's Palace, according to Ash Resnick, the house advantage is at about 20 per cent. But this does not mean—either downtown or on the Strip—that every machine in the establishment is set at the house's percentage. One machine may be at 95–5, while the one next to it may be set 80–20 ratio. It is up to the player to ferret out the more liberal machines and play accordingly. But remember that the house changes this return ratio on a machine from time to time. Nevertheless, the *overall* percentage for the house from all the machines over a *given period of time* remains fixed by the desires of the management of the casino.

Incidentally, most of the poor paying machines, with percentages to just under 50 per cent, are generally found in drugstores, beauty parlors, and other businesses not directly connected with the casinos. In the vernacular of the "slot" fraternity, a machine in which the payout is high is described as "loose," while one in which the payout is small, or poor, is said to be "tight."

A word of warning: Many people win a jackpot and do not collect the proper amount of money. This is not the casino's fault, but rather the player's failure to read properly. In most casinos the payoff of a jackpot is automatic. That is to say, the machine dumps out *all* the money due the player into the payoff trough. There are, however, some machines, especially in the downtown casinos, that do not have the automatic payoff system for large winnings. In such cases, the machine pays out only a *portion* of the jackpot and the change girl gives the rest. Therefore, it is wise, if the machine is not marked "Automatic Jackpot Payoffs," to check with a house employee as to the method of collecting your winnings.

While most machines pay for winning combinations on the center line only, a few machines state: three bars in *any* position *pays* a jackpot. Such machines usually do *not* drop their jackpot automatically. Thus, if you play one marked in this fashion and have *three bars in sight*, no matter what their position, call for a change girl to collect your winnings. Thousands of dollars are lost each year by players, either because they are unable to understand what they have read, or because they are ashamed to show their confusion and call over a house employee to explain the situation. Incidentally, it is customary after winning a jackpot—but *not* required—to insert a coin in the slot, pull the handle, and play off the jackpot combination. But do not do this until you are sure that you have received all the money due you.

Here is an important point to remember about slot machine etiquette: Once a player begins playing a particular machine, it is considered his, and it is unethical for anyone to do anything to interfere with his play. Even though he might leave the machine for a moment to obtain change, it is considered unplayable for other players. In order to indicate that the machine is in play, it is standard practice to mark it with a cup placed over the handle.

Violation of this code can lead to a great deal of unpleasantness. Incidentally, it is considered perfectly proper for a player to play two or more machines at one time in *most* casinos.

You Can't Beat the Slots

Many people are under the impression that a machine is fixed to pay off after a certain amount of money has been received by it and that if they keep playing long enough, they will hit the jackpot. They could not be more wrong.

All Las Vegas' experts are quick to tell those who think that they can foretell or guess when the jackpot will show, that it is IMPOSSIBLE. Not even the slot machine mechanic, who knows these devices inside and out, can tell which combinations will show in the little glass windows. Sure, slot machines are set, but they pay off according to laws of chance, and you can just as easily hit a jackpot with one play as with a thousand.

There are thousands of players who waste their time by standing silently while some person pours money into a slot and then jump in when he or she quits, because they think that the "one-armed bandit" is ready to pay off. Much to their regret, they learn that it does not always happen that way. Just because the odds on a standard three-reeler are theoretically 8,000 to 1, does not mean that the double jackpot must appear at any precise moment. The law of averages may indicate when it is supposed to happen, but the law of averages does not always do what it is supposed to. That is, a jackpot could appear in ten spins or fifty spins or 1,000 spins, 2,500 spins, 5,000 spins or even 10,000 spins. Nobody knows when Lady Luck will smile on the law of averages. It is possible, as we said previously, for you to put one coin in a slot and a jackpot to fall. According to the law of averages, that was the time for the jackpot to drop and you were just lucky enough to be playing the right machine when it occurred. Recently, at the Dunes Hotel, a $1 slot machine paid off two $5,000 jackpots in as many days. The chances of something like this happening are about a million to one, but things like this do occur in Las Vegas.

As was stated earlier, slot machines are set by mechanics to give *specific* winnings—not the time when the machine is going to pay.

Years ago, when slot machines were legal in many states and were plentiful in bars and clubs throughout the country, many were adjusted so that they never paid the big prizes advertised. Today, in Las Vegas, the machines state what can be won and they *do* pay off. When a state inspector comes around (and the casino operators never know when), the machines better pay exactly what they state they will. The inspector is empowered to walk up to any machine and say "Open it." If he finds the payoffs are not made correctly, he can close a casino. Actually, it would be very foolish for a casino to try to beat the public in this manner. It is *not* necessary. All the establishment has to do is open its doors, keep the bells ringing, and the public will pay the high price for the privilege of playing slot machines.

While all the experts who helped prepare this book agreed that slot machines should only be used to test your luck or pass the time—but not for real gambling—they do provide a great deal of fun to many thousands of players each year. The reason most visitors to Las Vegas play slot machines is that they know nothing of the other games in a casino, games like Twenty-One, Craps or Roulette, so they must invest some money in some form of risk. After all, how could a person visiting in Las Vegas go home saying that he did not gamble? It would be rather embarrassing. And of all casino games, the slots *appear* to be the easiest. Just insert your coin and pull the handle. The popularity and appeal of the slot machines will always be there, regardless of what our experts say.

Keno, Bingo, and Casino
Side Games

This chapter should really be titled, "Games You Shouldn't Play," since Keno, Bingo, and other games mentioned in it are some of the highest house-advantage ones in Las Vegas. But they are very simple to play. Each is purely a game of chance; no skill is required to gain an advantage over the house or another player. For these reasons, people will play highly disadvantageous games.

Keno

Keno has often been called the worst sucker game in Las Vegas. It is, however, one of the most popular. True, Keno has a terrific lure to the *uninitiated* because the payoff can be as high as $25,000 for a $1 investment.

The game is basically a Chinese lottery sport and is played by marking a Keno card which has eighty numbers printed on it, ten to a line. After you have selected the numbers you wish to play, the marked card is then taken to one of the Keno ticket writers, or dealers, who marks a duplicate of your card. He keeps the original and gives you the duplicate as your receipt.

You do not have to be in the Keno lounge to play the game. Keno girls, or runners, will gladly give you a ticket any place in the casino and get the duplicate of your ticket for you. Then at a scheduled time, the drawing begins. Twenty numbered plastic balls are selected at random from a cage by a vacuum system. As each ball is drawn, the number is flashed up by the game operator on electric display boards, which are enlarged versions of a Keno card. After the numbers have been chosen, payoffs are made in accordance with the established odds, just as in any other game of chance.

Basics of Spot Tickets. In Keno, you may select from one to fifteen numbers, or spots, and are paid in accordance to the number of winning spots you catch on your ticket. Let us assume, for example, that you decided to play a "1-spot" ticket for $1. (The minimum amount that can be wagered in Keno is 50 cents.) If your number is one of twenty drawn from the cage, you receive $3.20 ($2.20 winners). Should you play a "2-spot" ticket for $2 and both numbers show, you would receive $13. You would, of course, lose if none or only one number shows. Reproduced on the following pages are the basic Keno ticket payoffs from the "1-spot" to the "15-spot."

As can be seen from this payoff chart, it is possible to win if all numbers or a portion of the numbers you marked are called. On the "10-spot," you win $180 for your $1 if 7 of your 10 numbers are called. And if you catch all 10, the payoff is $25,000, which is the maximum regardless of how many more than ten numbers you may hit.

While the basic payoff schedule shows winning returns up to $5, there is no limit to the amount of money you can invest in a single ticket. Multiples of the various dollar bets do not increase the payoff when the maximum of $25,000 has been won, but they will increase the lesser pays. For instance, suppose you play a $1 "6-spot" and catch five numbers. Your pay would be $110. Played for $5 it would be $550, while at $10, the payoff would be $1,100. But the maximum amount payed out by house in any one game is $25,000. That is what is meant by the statement on the Keno ticket: "$25,000 limit to aggregate players each game." In other words, the house limits its total payoff for any single game to $25,000 regardless of the number of tickets sold. Thus, if there happened to be many players with winning tickets, they would not be paid off at the advertised rate but would have to divide the $25,000 total pot.

SPECIAL TICKETS

MARK ONE NUMBER—1.00 - 2.00 - 5.00

Catch One ....Pays 3.20

MARK 2 NUMBERS

Catch 2 Numbers ....Pays 13 for 1

MARK 3 NUMBERS

Catch 2 Numbers ....Free Play
Catch 3 Numbers ....Pays 47 for 1

MARK 4 NUMBERS

Catch 2 Numbers ....Free Play
Catch 3 Numbers ....Pays 5 for 1
Catch 4 Numbers ....Pays 118 for 1

MARK 5 NUMBERS

Play .50 - 1.00 - 2.50

Catch	.50 Ticket	1.00 Ticket	2.50 Ticket
3 Pays	1.50	3.00	7.50
4 Pays	13.00	26.00	65.00
5 Pays	166.00	332.00	830.00

MARK 6 NUMBERS

Play .50 - 1.00 - 2.00

Catch	.50 Ticket	1.00 Ticket	2.00 Ticket
3 Pays	.50	1.00	2.00
4 Pays	2.80	5.60	11.20
5 Pays	55.00	110.00	220.00
6 Pays	620.00	1,240.00	2,480.00

MARK 7 NUMBERS

Every Ticket Wins

Play .50 - 1.00 - 2.00

Catch	.50 Ticket	1.00 Ticket	2.00 Ticket
0 Pays	.50	1.00	2.00
1 Pays	.15	.30	.60
2 Pays	.15	.30	.60
3 Pays	.20	.40	.80
4 Pays	1.00	2.00	4.00
5 Pays	8.00	16.00	32.00
6 Pays	88.00	176.00	352.00
7 Pays	750.00	1,500.00	3,000.00

MARK 8 NUMBERS

(.50 MINIMUM)

(.50 Multiple)

Catch	.50 Ticket	1.00 Ticket	5.00 Ticket
4 Pays	.75	1.50	7.50
5 Pays	7.20	14.40	72.00
6 Pays	54.00	108.00	540.00
7 Pays	400.00	800.00	4,000.00
8 Pays	2,000.00	4,000.00	20,000.00

(2.60 Multiple)

Catch	2.60 Ticket	3.20 Ticket	6.40 Ticket
3 Pays	.25	.35	.70
4 Pays	3.95	5.00	10.00
5 Pays	37.15	46.45	92.90
6 Pays	258.70	323.40	646.80
7 Pays	2,250.00	2,769.25	5,538.50
8 Pays	7,500.00	9,230.75	18,461.50

MARK 9 NUMBERS

Play .35 - .50 - 1.00 - 1.05 - 5.00 - Etc.

Catch	.35 Ticket	.50 Ticket	1.00 Ticket	1.05 Ticket
4 Pays	.15	.20	.40	.45
5 Pays	1.80	2.55	5.10	5.40
6 Pays	17.80	25.40	50.80	53.40
7 Pays	110.70	158.10	316.20	332.10
8 Pays	1,000.00	1,428.60	2,857.20	3,000.00
9 Pays	2,250.00	3,214.30	6,428.60	6,750.00

9-SPOT WAYS

(Groups of 3)

9 Spots,	1 way	..........cost	.35
12 Spots,	4 ways	..........cost	1.40
15 Spots,	10 ways	..........cost	3.50
18 Spots,	20 ways	..........cost	7.00
21 Spots,	35 ways	..........cost	12.25
24 Spots,	56 ways	..........cost	19.60
27 Spots,	84 ways	..........cost	29.40
30 Spots,	120 ways	..........cost	42.00
33 Spots,	165 ways	..........cost	57.75
36 Spots,	220 ways	..........cost	77.00
39 Spots,	286 ways	..........cost	100.10
42 Spots,	364 ways	..........cost	127.40
45 Spots,	455 ways	..........cost	159.25
48 Spots,	560 ways	..........cost	196.00
51 Spots,	680 ways	..........cost	238.00
54 Spots,	816 ways	..........cost	285.60
57 Spots,	969 ways	..........cost	339.15
60 Spots,	1140 ways	..........cost	399.00

Keno ticket payoffs.

HIGH LOW TICKET, 12 SPOTS
3 GROUPS OF 4

	Rate .35	Rate .90	Rate 1.80
2-2-1	.20	.50	1.00
3-1-1	.25	.60	1.20
3-2-0	.30	.70	1.40
4-1-0	.35	.90	1.80
2-2-2	1.50	3.90	7.80
3-2-1	1.80	4.60	9.20
4-1-1	2.40	6.00	12.00
3-3-0	2.40	6.00	12.00
4-2-0	2.65	6.70	13.40
3-2-2	11.35	28.40	56.80
3-3-1	14.25	35.70	71.40
4-2-1	17.15	43.00	86.00
4-3-0	23.00	57.60	115.20
3-3-2	61.70	161.30	322.60
4-2-2	81.35	209.20	418.40
4-3-1	100.00	257.10	514.20
4-4-0	155.85	400.80	801.60
3-3-3	259.00	666.00	1,332.00
4-3-2	262.35	675.00	1,350.00
4-4-1	269.50	693.00	1,386.00
4-3-3	606.65	1,560.00	3,120.00
4-4-2	1,018.00	2,615.00	5,230.00
4-4-3	2,216.65	5,700.00	11,400.00
4-4-4	9,000.00	22,500.00	25,000.00

MARK 13 NUMBERS
Play .50 - 1.00 - 5.00

Catch	.50 Ticket	1.00 Ticket	5.00 Ticket
7 Pays	9.00	18.00	90.00
8 Pays	53.00	106.00	530.00
9 Pays	460.00	920.00	4,600.00
10 Pays	2,200.00	4,400.00	22,000.00
11 Pays	4,240.00	8,480.00	25,000.00
12 Pays	6,000.00	12,000.00	25,000.00
13 Pays	8,000.00	16,000.00	25,000.00

MARK 14 NUMBERS
Play .50 - 1.00 - 5.00

Catch	.50 Ticket	1.00 Ticket	5.00 Ticket
7 Pays	5.00	10.00	50.00
8 Pays	28.50	57.00	285.00
9 Pays	197.00	394.00	1,970.00
10 Pays	700.00	1,400.00	7,000.00
11 Pays	4,000.00	8,000.00	25,000.00
12 Pays	9,000.00	18,000.00	25,000.00
13 Pays	18,500.00	25,000.00	25,000.00
14 Pays	25,000.00	25,000.00	25,000.00

MARK 15 NUMBERS
Play .50 - 1.00 - 5.00

Catch	.50 Ticket	1.00 Ticket	5.00 Ticket
7 Pays	4.00	8.00	40.00
8 Pays	14.00	28.00	140.00
9 Pays	82.00	164.00	820.00
10 Pays	315.00	630.00	3,150.00
11 Pays	1,300.00	2,600.00	13,000.00
12 Pays	6,000.00	12,000.00	25,000.00
13 Pays	14,000.00	25,000.00	25,000.00
14 Pays	25,000.00	25,000.00	25,000.00
15 Pays	25,000.00	25,000.00	25,000.00

MARK 10 NUMBERS
Play .50 - 1.00 - 5.00

Catch	.50 Ticket	1.00 Ticket	5.00 Ticket
5 Pays	1.00	2.00	10.00
6 Pays	9.00	18.00	90.00
7 Pays	90.00	180.00	900.00
8 Pays	650.00	1,300.00	6,500.00
9 Pays	1,300.00	2,600.00	13,000.00
10 Pays	12,500.00	25,000.00	25,000.00

MARK 11 NUMBERS
Play .50 - 1.00 - 5.00

Catch	.50 Ticket	1.00 Ticket	5.00 Ticket
5 Pays	.50	1.00	5.00
6 Pays	5.00	10.00	50.00
7 Pays	38.00	76.00	380.00
8 Pays	242.00	484.00	2,420.00
9 Pays	768.00	1,536.00	7,680.00
10 Pays	2,318.00	4,636.00	23,180.00
11 Pays	12,500.00	25,000.00	25,000.00

MARK 12 NUMBERS
Play .50 - 1.00 - 5.00

Catch	.50 Ticket	1.00 Ticket	5.00 Ticket
5 Pays	.30	.60	3.00
6 Pays	2.60	5.20	26.00
7 Pays	18.70	37.40	187.00
8 Pays	106.00	212.00	1,060.00
9 Pays	374.00	748.00	3,740.00
10 Pays	1,026.00	2,052.00	10,260.00
11 Pays	3,166.00	6,322.00	25,000.00
12 Pays	12,500.00	25,000.00	25,000.00

Keno ticket payoffs (continued).

Filled-out Keno ticket.

In addition to regular Keno, several casinos have introduced "Bonus Specials." As you can see from the payoff schedule, the low pays are generally less, but the high ones are greater. "Bonus Specials" begin with "4-spot" tickets and a minimum investment of 55 cents.

Spot Ticket Combinations. There are an infinite variety of spot combinations that may be played. While it is impossible in this book to detail all of them, we will cover the more important ones.

It is possible to play more than one Keno game at a time, but employing only one ticket. For instance, the basic "9-spot" is a single group of nine numbers played as a single game. If you select twelve numbers or more, you may increase the number of "9-spots" that you play on this single ticket. This is accomplished by forming "combinations" of the numbers played.

In marking the single "9-spot" the intent is obvious, but in twelve numbers or more, your selections must be divided on the ticket into groups of three. Mark twelve numbers, and you divide them into four groups of three. This simply means that there are four different ways that you can group the individual sets of three numbers to catch a winner in nine numbers. As shown on the previous chart, the minimum cost of "12-spot, 4 ways" ticket (35 cents minimum for a "9-spot") is $1.40 (4 times 35 cents).

In the Keno ticket shown on page 140, you will note that the selections have been placed into four groups of three, as previously explained. The division may be any way you choose and the numbers any twelve you prefer, but they must eventually represent four groups of three numbers each and the division must be shown in your markings on the original ticket. In our example, the selections are grouped as follows:

9, 10, 19 (one group)
12, 13, 34 (one group)
37, 59, 69 (one group)
71, 72, 73 (one group)

Suppose that the following winning numbers are drawn: 12, 13, 19, 71, and 73. Here is what we have won and why.

First check the pay schedule for a "9-spot" ticket. Remember that this ticket represents a "9-spot" played four different ways; then you know there are four possible ways to win. Combine the four groups of three as follows:

Employing 9, 10, 19 and 12, 13, 34 and 71, 72, 73, there are five winning numbers: 12, 13, 19, 71 and 73. This represents five winners out of nine numbers and the payoff is $1.80. With 12, 13, 34 and 37, 59, 69 and 71, 72, 73, there are four winning numbers: 12, 13, 71, and 73. This is four winners and good for 15 cents payoff. Grouping 9, 10, 19 and 12, 13, 34 and 37, 59, 69 produces three winning numbers. Three numbers do not pay. Finally, with 9, 10, 19 and 37, 59, 69 and 71, 72, 73, again there are three winning numbers only and no payoff. Total payoff on this ticket which cost $1.40 is $2.05 and wins 65 cents. As you can see, additional winning numbers in any or all of the four groups will greatly increase both the number of pays and the amount of winnings.

Cost is based on multiples of the minimum or the selected unit for a single play. When you mark sixty spots, for example, you increase your possibility of winning to 1,140 ways on a "9-spot," but the cost of such a ticket at the 35 cent rate is $399 (1,140 times 35 cents). While the "9-spot" ways is the most popular, some casinos have recently instituted the "8-spot" ways (groups of four) and "10-spot" ways (groups of five). These are played in a manner similar to the "9-spot" ways, except that the groupings are different.

Another interesting variation in Keno is a so-called "high-low" ticket. On such a "12-spot" ticket you mark three groups of four numbers each. For purposes of following the play more easily, let us group the numbers as follows: Group I: 7, 8, 9, 10; Group II: 14, 25, 26, 37; Group III: 41, 53, 61, 73; and Group IV: 48, 58, 67, 69. Now, assume the ticket catches the following winning numbers: 9, 10, 14, 25, 37, and 61. Any numerical combination in any three of the groups above that represents the "high." By checking the different groups, you can see that there are two winning numbers in Group I, three winning numbers in Group II, one winning number in Group III, and no winning numbers in Group IV. Selecting your highest combination in three of the four groups, you arrive at: 3–2–1. By checking the pay chart here, you will notice that this combination pays $4.60 for a 90 cents ticket.

Keno runners are for your convenience. We are not responsible if tickets are too late for game played.

SPECIAL BONUS TICKETS COSTS AND PAY OFFS

SPECIAL — 4 — SPOTS

Catch	Play 55¢	Play $1.10	Play $5.50
3—Win	$ 2.50	$ 5.00	$ 25.00
4—Win	100.00	200.00	1,000.00

SPECIAL — 5 — SPOTS

Catch	Play 55¢	Play $1.10	Play $5.50
3—Win	$ 1.00	$ 2.00	$ 10.00
4—Win	13.00	26.00	130.00
5—Win	280.00	560.00	2,800.00

SPECIAL — 6 — SPOTS

Catch	Play 55¢	Play $1.10	Play $5.50
4—Win	$ 4.00	$ 8.00	$ 40.00
5—Win	55.00	110.00	550.00
6—Win	1,000.00	2,000.00	10,000.00

SPECIAL — 7 — SPOTS

Catch	Play 55¢	Play $1.10	Play $5.50
4—Win	$ 1.50	$ 3.00	$ 15.00
5—Win	13.00	26.00	130.00
6—Win	200.00	400.00	2,000.00
7—Win	3,000.00	6,000.00	25,000.00

SPECIAL — 8 — SPOTS

Catch	Play 55¢	Play $1.10	Play $5.50
5—Win	$ 5.00	$ 10.00	$ 50.00
6—Win	45.00	90.00	450.00
7—Win	1,100.00	2,200.00	11,000.00
8—Win	12,500.00	25,000.00	25,000.00

SPECIAL — 9 — SPOTS

Catch	Play 55¢	Play $1.10	Play $5.50
5—Win	$ 2.00	$ 4.00	$ 20.00
6—Win	27.00	54.00	270.00
7—Win	175.00	350.00	1,750.00
8—Win	3,000.00	6,000.00	25,000.00
9—Win	11,000.00	22,000.00	25,000.00

SPECIAL — 10 — SPOTS

Catch	Play 55¢	Play $1.10	Play $5.50
6—Win	$ 10.00	$ 20.00	$ 100.00
7—Win	100.00	200.00	1,000.00
8—Win	900.00	1,800.00	9,000.00
9—Win	4,000.00	8,000.00	25,000.00
10—Win	16,000.00	25,000.00	25,000.00

SPECIAL — 11 — SPOTS

Catch	Play 55¢	Play $1.10	Play $5.50
6—Win	$ 5.00	$ 10.00	$ 50.00
7—Win	40.00	80.00	400.00
8—Win	300.00	600.00	3,000.00
9—Win	1,400.00	2,800.00	14,000.00
10—Win	5,000.00	10,000.00	25,000.00
11—Win	20,000.00	25,000.00	25,000.00

YOU CAN PLAY KENO WHILE IN THE BAR OR RESTAURANT

Bonus Specials payoffs.

Keno and the Odds

There is an almost limitless variety of combinations that can be played on a single Keno ticket. But in spite of this, it is still one of the biggest sucker games in Las Vegas. The mathematics of computing your chances of winning money and the cost of playing Keno are fairly simple. On a "1-spot" ticket, for example, the possibility of your selecting the correct number to be drawn from the twenty (out of eighty) is exactly 20/80, or ½. However, the house pays you $3.20 for $1, meaning that you risked one betting unit (the price of your ticket) to win $2.20 more. You should have won three at correct odds, and the house percentage is 20. The following table shows the percentages in favor of the house on all tickets from the "1-spot" through the "15-spot," calculated on the payoff price given on pages 138–39:

Ticket	House Percentage	Ticket	House Percentage
1 spot	20.0%	9 spot	21.3%
2 spot	21.8%	10 spot	20.6%
3 spot	20.9%	11 spot	20.2%
4 spot	21.0%	12 spot	20.1%
5 spot	22.0%	13 spot	21.1%
6 spot	21.0%	14 spot	20.7%
7 spot	19.5%	15 spot	21.2%
8 spot	21.3%		

To go into complete detail about all of the mathematical odds affecting payoffs on all of the different Keno tickets would fill a book bigger than this one. But we would like to show the payoff and actual odds on the "10-spot" ticket, the most popular one at Las Vegas.

Number of Catches	Payoff on $1 Ticket	Payoff Odds	Actual Odds
1 to 4	No Payoff	—	—
5	$2.00	2–1	18–1
6	$18.00	18–1	86–1
7	$180.00	180–1	620–1
8	$1,300.00	1,300–1	7,380–1
9	$2,600.00	2,600–1	163,380–1
10	$25,000.00	25,000–1	8,911,710–1

In addition to exacting a tax of better than 20 cents out of each $1 bet, the house also has the $25,000-limit aggregate payoff rule going for it. Because of the obvious disadvantage to the player, Major A. Riddle, president of the Dunes Hotel, gives the following advice: "If you plan to play Keno, give the money to charity instead, because you can count on being parted from it, and a gift to charity might give you some satisfaction whereas losing money at Keno won't."

Bingo

Bingo is a "kissing-cousin" to Keno, and its house percentage is probably at least as atrocious, and quite possibly a little worse. The mechanics of the game make it very difficult to gather accurate information on the house's cut. While Bingo could *not* be considered a major game in Las Vegas, nevertheless it has its followers, especially among the women.

Bingo is played in Nevada in the same manner as it is in the other forty-nine states, except here it is completely legal to play for money prizes. The first step in the game's play is to purchase one or more printed Bingo cards that contain a five-by-five array of numbers, except that the center square in the array is marked *free play*. That is, the first column contains five different numbers chosen at random from 1 through 15, the second column has five more from 16 through 30, the third column contains only four numbers from 31 through 45, plus the free play square. The other two columns contain five numbers apiece, thus twenty-four of the seventy-five numbers used in the game appear on a card.

Once all the participants have purchased their cards and the game is determined ready for play, the "caller" draws numbers at random, using the same type of device used in Keno; that is, numbered plastic balls in a whirling cage. As the balls are selected, the caller announces them over a public address system and pushes a button which illuminates the chosen number on a board in plain view of all players in the Bingo parlor.

As the winning numbers are called one by one, each player places a marker on any winning number that appears on his card. (Most modern-day Bingo cards have self-contained tabs used to cover the called numbers, eliminating the need for markers.) As soon as a player covers five numbers in any row, horizontally, vertically, or diagonally, or four numbers plus the free play, he calls out "Bingo." Play is then halted while a casino agent checks the card by reading off the winning numbers. If no error exists, the game is over and the player is paid. If an error does occur, the game is continued until a valid card is found.

Like Keno, there are seemingly endless variations of the game. Three of the most common are the "T," "X," and "Diamond" games. In the "T" game, the numbers covered must form the letter "T" on the cards. The "X" game is played the same way; that is the letter "X" must be formed on the card to produce a winner. The "Diamond" game requires that numbers be covered in the pattern of a diamond.

Different prices are charged for cards with different colors. The value of the color may vary from Bingo parlor to Bingo parlor, but the basic premise is the same. One color may be sold at three cards for 10 cents, another at three cards for 25 cents, and so on. You may buy as many cards as you wish; these purchases are made in advance of the game. In the event that a series of games is played, the purchase may be made for the entire series. If you buy six or more cards of one or mixed colors, you will receive a "bonus card," usually gold in color and referred to as a gold card. This card pays double, or a special jackpot, if the game is won on it. Incidentally, a complete deck of Bingo cards contains 3,250 cards with no duplicate number combinations. The prize in regular Bingo usually averages from $10 to $200 per game. Special bonus and jackpot prizes may range from $500 to $5,000.

As previously stated, it is almost impossible, because of the number of variables—amount of prizes, number of players, cost of cards, etc.—to make a direct computation of the house percentage. However, all the Las Vegas casino operators that we talked with agreed that the house advantage is high—at least 20 per cent.

Casino Side Games

In addition to the regular, or major, games like Craps, Blackjack, Roulette, Slot Machines, and Keno, many casinos have one or more minor banking games known as side games. At Las Vegas, these games include the Money Wheel, the Big Six, and Chuck-a-Luck.

The Money Wheel

The Money Wheel, or Wheel of Fortune as it sometimes is called, is a giant wheel of chance five feet in diameter which, with its pedestal, stands eight feet high. The rim of the wheel is divided into fifty-four sections covered with glass, and in fifty-two of these are dollar bills in denominations of one to twenty. (There are twenty-four $1 bills, fifteen $2 bills, seven $5 bills, four $10 bills and two $20 bills.) The remaining two sections bear a picture of a Flag or the casino name, and a Joker. The betting layout has one each of these items—$1, $2, $5, $10, $20, Flag and Joker—encased in glass.

The player places his money on one or more spaces on the betting layout and then the dealer spins the wheel in a clockwise direction. Projecting posts (nails) on the outer edge of the wheel's rim separate the spaces and pass by a leather indicator at the top. When the wheel comes to a stop, the section in which the indicator rests is the winner. The value of the bill in that section indicates the payoff odds to the winner. That is, the $1 bill has a 1 to 1 payoff, the $2 bill a 2 to 1 payoff, and so forth. The Joker and the other insignia pay 40 to 1, but the wager must be on the winning insignia to be paid. The usual minimum wager is 25 cents downtown and $1 on the Strip.

Some Money Wheel players think that the big odds offered cut down the operator's edge, and some even believe that the game is almost dead even. This logic can be put aside by a quick study of the following chart:

Bill or Insignia	Payoff Odds	Actual Odds	House's Advantage
$1	1 to 1	53 to 24	11.1%
$2	2 to 1	53 to 15	16.7%
$5	5 to 1	53 to 7	25.9%
$10	10 to 1	53 to 4	18.5%
$20	20 to 1	53 to 2	22.3%
Flag	40 to 1	53 to 1	24.1%
Joker	40 to 1	53 to 1	24.1%

There are several Money Wheels in Las Vegas that have fifty sections—and even a couple with forty-eight divisions—instead of fifty-four. While the odds do change slightly in favor of the player on these smaller wheels, the $1 bill remains the "best bet," if the term could be applied to any money wheel wagers.

While the wheels in Las Vegas are *not* rigged, it is possible for an experienced dealer to exert some influence on the outcome of the spin. By carefully timing the spin, it is possible to stop the wheel in any given quarter. Since the Flag and Joker are 180 degrees apart, a dealer could keep the wheel from the 40 to 1 payoffs. To prevent this, most casinos require that their Money Wheel dealers spin without looking at the wheel or timing its action.

The Big Six

The mechanical structure and rules of play of Big Six are very much like the Money Wheel except that it uses a different betting layout. On each of the fifty-four spaces around the wheel's rim show one side of three dice bearing different combinations of the numbers 1 through 6 in which six have no pairs, twenty-four have pairs and twenty-four have three of a kind. There is a layout which also bears the numbers 1 through 6.

The mechanics of the game are simple. The players place their bets (a minimum of 25 cents downtown and $1 on the Strip) on the numbers on the layout. Then the dealer spins the wheel and pays off all the winning numbers according to the number of times they appear on the wheel. For instance, suppose you place $1 on 2 and the wheel stops at 1–2–3, you receive $1 plus the $1 you invested since the 2 showed only once. But, if the wheel had stopped at 2–2–3, you would have gotten $2 plus your original $1 since the 2 showed up twice on the winning combination. If the wheel had stopped at 2–2–2, you would have received $3 and your $1. While the odds may *seem* good, the house percentage is about 20 per cent, which means stay away from Big Six unless you wish to help along the casino's profits. Even some Big Six wheels have fewer than fifty-four sections—fifty or forty or some other number —and the dice arrangements on their winning sections vary as well. But remember that the more triplets there are on the wheel, the greater the house's percentage.

There are other wheels of chance games available in Las Vegas; the casino's favorable edge ranges from as low as 15 to as high as 25 per cent. They may be fun to play, but *never* expect to win any money at any of them.

Chuck-a-Luck

Chuck-a-Luck is the game from which Big Six is derived. It is a simple game in which three dice are tumbled over and over in a cage until they come to rest. Before the cage is turned, the players place their bets on a layout divided into six squares and numbered 1 through 6 (almost the same identical layout used for Big Six). The house pays various odds on the bets corresponding to those shown on the dice. For instance, if the player's selected number appears on all three dice, he is paid at 3 to 1. If it appears on two of the three dice, the payoff is 2 to 1, and if it shows on one of the dice, the payoff is 1 to 1. If none of the three dice bears his number, he loses. While some naïve players think that they have the best of it, the odds are 216 to 199 in favor of the house, or a 7.9 per cent advantage. (There are 216 different combinations that the three dice can make—$6 \times 6 \times 6 = 216$. There are ninety combinations that can make pairs, six combinations that can make three of a kind, and only 120 combinations that consist of no pairs.)

In a few Chuck-a-Luck games there are other bets. For example, the house pays even money on *High* (total 11 to 17), *Low* (total 4 to 10), *Odd* and *Even* numbers. But the house wins whenever a triple shows in the High and Low bets. For instance, 15 loses if 5–5–5 comes up, and 9 loses if 3–3–3 comes up. Still these are the best bets for the player. The correct odds are only 111 to 105 against him, or a house percentage of 2.8 per cent.

If you bet that the next tumbling of the cage will produce triples (called raffles), such as 2–2–2 or 4–4–4, the house pays 30 to 1. But the actual odds are 35 to 1 or a house advantage of 13.9 per cent. You can also bet on a particular triple or raffle, and if it comes up, the house pays 180 to 1. Great odds? No—not when you consider the correct odds or chances of making it are 215 to 1. The house percentage is thus 16.2 per cent.

You can also bet on any given total, from 4 to 17. The payoffs on the various combinations of numbers are as follows:

Combination	Payoff Odds	Actual Odds	House's Advantage
4 or 17	60 to 1	71 to 1	15.3%
5 or 16	30 to 1	35 to 1	13.9%
6 or 15	23 to 1	18 to 1	20.8%
7 or 14	12 to 1	67 to 5	9.7%
8 or 13	8 to 1	65 to 7	12.5%
9 or 12	6 to 1	8 to 1	22.2%
10 or 11	6 to 1	7 to 1	12.5%

Actually, this game should be called "Chuck-Away-Your-Bucks." It is not hard to understand why Chuck-a-Luck's general popularity is on the decline—along with the Money Wheel and Bingo—in Las Vegas. Actually, the only "big" house advantage games that are increasing in popularity are Keno and the Slot Machines.

9

♠

Betting on Horse Races and Sporting Events

Nevada is the only state in the United States where off-track betting and sports bookmaking are legal. In most cases, Las Vegas' horse betting establishments are run in conjunction with sports book-making. Nevada gambling officials exercise as strict control over these establishments as they do the casinos. But, despite the fact that the number of casinos is on the increase, the average racing and sports clubs are on the decline. The reason is simply that the appeal to the big gambler for the opportunity to make a *legal* bet on any sporting event is dampened by the 10 per cent Federal excise tax that he must pay.

In 1951, Congress passed a law which it thought would suppress off-track and sports betting by requiring all bookies to buy a $50 gambling stamp and pay a 10 per cent excise tax on their gross receipts. In all states except Nevada, however, betting on horses at any place other than the track is illegal. So the only state that the 1951 Federal law affects *legally* is Nevada. In addition, the state of Nevada requires that a horse and sports book must be operated in a building separated from all other forms of gambling. The bookies must all pay an annual 3 per cent state tax on gross winnings under $250,000, a slightly higher tax on a gross over that. So far, no Nevada race and sports book has as yet reported winnings exceeding $250,000.

Actually, it seems rather hypocritical that the only legitimate bookmakers in our country are having difficulties to stay in business because of the special Federal tax. Illegitimate bookies, of course, do not pay this tax and their business is flourishing. Thus, the great prosperity of the illegal bookmaking industry, in spite of all attempts by Federal and state governments to suppress it, is definite proof that the millions and millions of Americans who bet on horse races and sporting events are not in full accord with the present anti-bookmaking statutes.

Let us take a look at a typical Las Vegas race and sports book. For instance, you can go out on the Strip, past the Dunes and the Sands hotels, and find a small building with bright red letters—Race Book—on the roof. The full name is on the windows in yellow and blue paint: "Santa Anita Turf and Sports Club." The sign on the door says: "No minors allowed. Closed Sundays."

Inside, it is a very clean place and surprisingly bright. The big board with the entries from the major race tracks across the United States stretches the full length of one wall. Under the big board are the cashier cages. The large room accommodates about 250 customers who sit at the kind of plastic-topped tables you see at lunch counters. All of them are quiet, all of them seem to be reading their free copies of the *Daily Racing Form* or watching the big board in front of them.

"A lot of our customers are women, so we do not tolerate any bad language," said Sammy Cohen, owner of the Club.

Horse Racing

At most Las Vegas "betting parlors," the main business is horses and the sports book is run as an accommodation to their customers. Before the advent of pari-mutuel betting, of course, bookmakers operated openly and within the law at all legal race tracks. But the use of pari-mutuel machines (automatic ticket sellers and the totalizator) has eliminated the need for a bookmaker to make book at a track. Away from the track (off-track), he is necessary to take bets and to pay off to winners.

In this book we cannot go into details of horse race betting and the many systems employed by horse players. There are several excellent books on the subject listed in Appendix B. We will cover, however, the differences between betting at the track and at one of Las Vegas' race books.

Betting

Just as at the track, there are three major money pools in each race covered by the book: win, place and show. The payoff prices at the track under the pari-mutuel betting system for each pool depends entirely on the total amount of money bet to win, place and show, and the amount wagered on the horses that finish first, second and third. At most of Las Vegas' race books, full track odds are payed up to $5 across the board. The limits on the balance are: win—15 to 1; place—6 to 1; and show 3 to 1. Entries and field bets go as one unless otherwise specified.

Race books in Las Vegas usually provide for bets being made on any horse in a race in one or all of the following nine ways:

1. *To win.* The bettor collects when the horse he wagered to win finishes first.

2. *To place.* The bettor collects when the horse he wagered to place finishes either first or second.

3. *To show.* The bettor collects when the horse he wagered to show finishes either first, second, or third.

4. *Daily Double.* The bettor collects when the horses he wagered to win in the first and second races both finish first. The daily double at the Las Vegas books is usually limited to 50 to 1 on all Eastern tracks, 100 to 1 on all California tracks. There are no consolation doubles; if one horse is scratched your money is refunded. A few books are now offering twin daily doubles which involve the four winning horses in four different races (usually the first two and last two races). The twin, in every sense of the word, is an extension of the daily double.

5. *Parlay.* The bettor collects when the horses he wagered to either win, place, or show in two or more races come in the way he predicted. That is, if one horse finishes in the designated position or better (in the case of place or show bets), the original wager, plus the winnings, automatically becomes the bet on the other horse or horses in the parlay. When one or more horses in a parlay do not start, the player receives the payoff price produced by the

horse or horses that run, unless otherwise stipulated. Parlays are limited to 100 to 1. All parlays at most books, are figured on the basis of: win—15 to 1; place—6 to 1; and show—3 to 1.

6. *Quinella.* The bettor collects when the two horses he wagers on in one race finished first and second, without regard to the order in which they did so.

7. *Double Quinella.* This is a separate pool and is divided equally between the holders of winning tickets. All four horses on a winning ticket must finish first and second or second and first in the two races designated by the race book. In the event of any scratches in a double quinella, the money is refunded and deducted from the pool. In the event of a dead heat for the first or second position in either race of the double quinella, the pool will be divided equally among the winning ticket holders regardless of the mutuels. In the event there are no winning tickets on the four horses finishing first and second or second and first in the two halves of the double quinella, usually 70 per cent of the day's pool is added to the next day's pool for the double quinella betting. (A pool limit of generally $1,500 is set.) Incidentally, the double quinella payoff is based on a $2 ticket. Entries and field horses run separately in all quinella betting.

8. *Perfecta.* The bettor collects when the two horses he wagers on in one race finish *exactly* in the manner he selected. In other words, perfecta betting is similar to quinella except that the order of finish of the two horses the player chooses must be perfect. While quinella betting is offered generally on all races on the book's big board, perfecta, at the present time, is limited to Florida race tracks and on races selected by the track. The race books' limits on a perfecta is usually 100–1; the general payoff is based on the track odds.

9. *Future Book.* Some Las Vegas race books list all horses nominated for a stakes race (usually the triple crown races) well in advance of the actual running and accept wagers at stipulated odds. Payoffs to the winners are made according to those odds, regardless of the eventual totalisator track prices. If a horse fails to start for any reason, all bets on that horse are forfeit to the book.

Remember that the Federal tax of 10 per cent of the amount wagered is collected at the time the bet is made. For example, to make a $2 bet, you must give the cashier $2.20. Speaking of the cashier, always check your tickets before leaving the counter. The management is not responsible for errors unless they are reported immediately. Also do not destroy any tickets until a race is declared "official" on the big board. If a foul claim is allowed, your ticket is valuable in the event of a disqualification out of a *win* position. Up to the first $10 wagered to win, the race book will usually pay on only disqualified win tickets at the odds quoted in the *Daily Racing Form* charts on the following day. (This offer is generally void on daily doubles, parlays, all quinellas, or any race not posted on the book's boards.) Disqualification payoffs are at full track odds up to $5, 15 to 1 for the next $5.

It is wise when wagering at a race book to stick to the first three bets: win, place and show. Daily doubles, parlays, quinellas, perfectas, future books, or any of the other forms of betting pools, such as five-and-tens and round-robins, are "bad" bets. True, they occasionally produce big payoffs; however, as previously stated, all race books have limits which they pay. Because of the extra-hazardous nature of these bets it is best to stay with the three conventional wagers.

Another interesting point to keep in mind is that recent computer studies show up the fallacy of the "safety" of the place or show bets. Most old-time race players considered place or show betting more profitable in the long run than wagering to win only. While a capable handicapper will always have a larger number of place or show selections than win choices, the substantially lower payoffs resulting from successful place and show bets will produce a lower overall return than the same amounts bet on the same horses to win only. If you do not believe this statement, make, over a period of weeks, 50 "mind bets" on horses to place, show or both. Then note the win prices of those horses that actually won, and compare the total win, place and show payoffs for all horses played. The results may surprise you.

Selecting the Horses

We are not going into the mechanics of selecting a horse. Las Vegas is not the place to learn this. The *Daily Racing Form*, which is generally given free by the race book, is the valuable tool in choosing a horse to bet. This publication gives all the pertinent data necessary for the competent horse player to make his selection. For instance, almost all the facts needed to properly evaluate the chances of any one horse against the other horse in a particular race can be quickly found in the publication's "past performances" chart for that race. After the race has been run, the "official result" charts tell the complete story of the event. If you studiously apply yourself to coordinating the information contained in these charts, plus a *very* careful evaluation of the choices of the public handicappers that appear in the newspapers, you will be well on your way to learning "how to win" in a race book at Las Vegas.

But when wagering at a Las Vegas betting establishment, remember the basic facts of money management given in Chapter 2. This information holds good when taking part in any phase of the sport of gambling. Incidentally, racing "systems" are no better than other betting systems discussed earlier. No betting system is worth the paper it is written on.

Sports Events

Sports Illustrated Magazine estimated recently that $7 billion a year is wagered with illegal bookmakers in the United States. Of that almost half is placed on the sports world's Big Three—baseball, football and basketball. Betting on these sports, of course, is illegal in all states except Nevada. The funny part about this situation is that very little money, percentage-wise, is bet on sports in Las Vegas. As we stated earlier, sports books are run as accommodations in most horse betting parlors.

Baseball

On the front wall of the race book you will find a space marked "Official Baseball Line." Under it, there are odds on all the baseball games to be played that day, determined by the race book's handicapper, or from sports services which sell this information to bookies throughout the country. They may read for a specific day something like this:

Mets 6½–7½ over Astros; Giants 6½–7½ over Phils; Braves-Reds pick 'em; Pirates 5–6 over Dodgers; Cards 7–8 over Cubs.

Angels 6–7 over Yanks; Tigers even–6 over Red Sox; Twins 8–9 over Senators; White Sox-Indians pick 'em; Orioles-A's pick 'em.

In betting on any sporting event, a gambler generally wins or loses in direct proportion to his knowledge of the sport and his ability to properly estimate the odds quoted. Unfortunately, the average bettor unknowingly permits his emotions to temper his judgment. Statistics on games of chance which involve inanimate objects such as cards or dice or machines like the roulette wheel are an exact science, but when research embraces human performance its literal interpretation always entails a considered risk. A professional gambler will never misfigure the odds on the toss of the dice or a spin of the roulette wheel, but when he applies the same computer-like logic to the behavior of an athlete or a team of athletes, he can make an error. Actually what makes him vulnerable is his inability to cope with the psychological factor.

"You don't have to be a player to know all about the game," said Sammy Cohen. "I'd bet my bankroll that guys like Jimmy 'The Greek' Snyder and my sports handicapper, Nat Lurie, could show any major-league baseball manager or football coach a thing or two." And after carefully analyzing the methods used by the two men Cohen mentioned in compiling the odds on sporting events, we are convinced that he is right. Were it not for the fact that sports handicappers have to disregard to a degree the psychological factor, they would be next to impossible to beat.

A professional baseball analyst, such as Nat Lurie, works on the premise that when two major-league teams meet, the mathematical chance of one defeating the other is based on four separate and distinct factors: offense, defense, pitching, and whether the team is playing "at home" or "away." These factors are not of equal value. Pitching ranks first by a wide margin.

Because of the importance of pitching, the difference between two competing pitchers' rating is always a fair barometer of about what the odds will be. In some sport clubs, the pitchers and their records are listed on the big board. Here is the information as it appeared on June 19, 1968:

Club	Pitcher	1968 Record	1968 vs. Club	Lifetime vs. Club	Odds
Astros	Wilson (R)	4–8	0–0	2–0	6½
Mets	Koosman (L)	10–2	1–0	1–1	7½
Giants	Marichal (R)	12–2	3–0	18–10	7½
Phillies	L. Jackson (R)	6–6	1–0	23–28	6½
Reds	McCool (L)	3–3	0–0	5–3	EVEN
Braves	Kelley (L)	2–4	1–0	1–3	
Dodgers	Singer (R)	6–5	2–0	3–1	6
Pirates	Veale (L)	4–7	0–2	12–8	7
Cubs	Nye (L)	4–6	0–0	1–4	7
Cardinals	Carlton (L)	7–2	1–0	3–1	8
Yankees	Barber (L)	0–1	0–0	12–6	6
Angels	Ellis (R)	3–5	0–0	0–0	5
Red Sox	Bell (R)	5–2	1–0	14–14	EVEN
Tigers	Sparma (R)	5–6	1–1	4–8	
Senators	Coleman (R)	4–6	1–0	1–3	8
Twins	Chance (R)	5–8	1–1	10–5	9
Indians	Tiant (R)	9–5	2–0	7–4	EVEN
White Sox	John (L)	5–0	0–0	5–5	
Orioles	Bunker (R)	0–0	0–0	9–4	EVEN
Athletics	Hunter (R)	5–5	0–2	7–6	

If you wish, it is possible to bet on the pitchers rather than teams. That is, if either of the pitchers listed on the board does not start the bet is off. If you still wish to bet on a team regardless of the pitcher, you may do so at the "Official Line" prices.

Like the casinos, the sports club operators must obtain a favorable percentage on every bet he accepts, no matter which team the player puts his money on. The Las Vegas Books generally offer two price lines, depending on the amount the customer wishes to bet. For the average bettor, $1 to $100, there is the so-called 20 cents line, while for the big bettor, $100 or more on a single bet, there is the 10 cents line.

The 20 cents line is based on a one-point odd spread, or a 20 cents spread when based on a $1 take price. The sports book's favorable percentage, or advantage, on this line ranges anywhere from a little over 1 per cent upwards to 6 per cent depending on the actual bet. Let us take a look at two examples that show the one-point differential and the 20 cents difference between the sports book's take and lay price.

As you know when two ball teams are rated at even money, or pick 'em, it means that each team is considered to have an equal chance of winning. But in such cases you do not put up an equal amount of money with the book. When a baseball game is quoted as even money on the 20 cents line, the book quotes a price of 5½ to 5 pick 'em. The customer must lay $1.10 to the book's $1, no matter which team he selects to win.

For example, referring to the "Official Baseball Line" given earlier in this chapter, you will find in the case of the Twins and Senators game that the Twins are an 8½ to 5 favorite. But the 20 cents price "official" line reads: "8–9 Twins favorite," which means that the sports book will lay on the Twins at $1.60 to $1 or take the Senators if the customer wagers $1.80 to $1. One point you must remember is that the 10 per cent Federal tax must be added to the bet. In the latter case, this means $1.98 to $1.

As we stated previously, the 10 cents line is given only on wagers of more than $100. This line operates on ½ of one point differential between the book's lay and take price. On an even-money or pick 'em wager, the customer must lay the book odds of 5¼ to 5, rather than the 5½ to 5 odds of the 20 cents line. If a ball team is a 6 to 5 favorite, the sports book will lay the customer odds of 5¾ to 5 and require that the customer lay him odds of 6¼ to 5. The 5¼ pick 'em is really a $1.05 to $1 wager, while the 6¼ to 5 is $1.20 to $1. Incidentally, the book's percentage advantage on the 10 cents line is from just under 1 per cent to over 5 per cent.

On the 10 cents line you will often note that the official line may read "Pirates favorite 120–130," or maybe just say "20–30." This means that the book will lay $1.20 to $1 on the Pirates, and if the customer wants to bet on the Pirates in their game against the Dodgers, for instance, he must lay the book $1.30 to $1. By the way, most 10 cents line bets are based primarily on the starting pitcher as recorded on the sports book's big board. If one pitcher does not start as indicated, all bets can be cancelled.

Each year at the beginning of the baseball season the various sports clubs set the odds on the two pennant races. As the season progresses, the odds on the various teams vary according to their play. The Las Vegas odds and prices on the pennant races and World Series are well known throughout the baseball world and are often quoted by sports writers.

Football

Betting on both college and professional football games has been on the increase in Las Vegas and throughout the country. In the "fun capital of the United States," the sports book that handles baseball action also usually handles the football bets.

The scouting systems and methods used by the sports services who inform the Las Vegas books on the various football games would make the C.I.A. look like a bunch of Boy Scouts. They seem to know everything about the two teams that are facing each other. After this data is carefully digested, the pricemakers set a suitable point spread or handicap which he thinks will equalize each opposing team's chance of winning, as far as the book and the customer are concerned.

In the annual Southern California–Notre Dame game, for example, after the pricemaker makes a careful study of the scouting material on both teams, he decides that Southern Cal should beat the Fighting Irish by 7 points. That is, he makes the game an even-money contest by quoting a price line of "Southern California 7 points over Notre Dame." This means that the bettors who put their money on U.S.C. win their wagers if Southern Cal beats Notre Dame by a margin of 8 points or more. If Southern California wins by exactly 7 points the game is considered a standoff (a tie) and the bettor neither wins nor loses. Should U.S.C. beat Notre Dame by 6 or less, or if Notre Dame should win, then all wagers on Southern California are lost.

When the pricemaker believes that the two opposing teams are evenly matched, most of Las Vegas' sport books' line will *usually* read "Southern California–Notre Dame pick 'em 11–10." In such cases, neither team is given any points or handicap. The bet, however, is not made at even money. You may select either team, but must lay the book the odds. The 11 to 10 line gives the sports book a percentage advantage of 4.55 per cent.

In recent years, to reduce the possibility of standoffs, the price-maker may use a half-point differential. That is, the price line may read: "Southern California 7½ points over Notre Dame." This half point is also employed as a come-on to induce bettors to wager on the underdog and as a means of price changing. Actually the price, or odds, changes frequently before a football contest. Before the professional Super Bowl game in 1968, for example, Sammy Cohen told us that the point spread changed six or seven times a day. "The Saturday before the game," said Cohen, "it started at 12½ points, jumped to 14, and ended at 13½. The flow of money guides us always. If we're out of line, money talks. The 12½ points was gobbled up by bettors who liked Oakland, so we pushed it up to 14 points. Then came some Packer money, so we dropped it to 13½."

Basketball

Basketball has never received the popularity among the gamblers that baseball and football have. For this reason, most Las Vegas sporting books do not handle basketball bets.

In the few books that offer a basketball line, the point differential system, which is just like the football line, is used. If U.C.L.A. is a 6-point favorite over Houston and you bet on U.C.L.A., for example, you collect only if U.C.L.A. beats Houston by 7 points or more. If U.C.L.A. wins by exactly 6 points, the game is considered a standoff and all bets are off. If U.C.L.A. wins by 5 points or less, or if the University of Houston wins, all wagers on U.C.L.A. are lost.

Other Sports

Because of the number of championship tournaments held in Las Vegas each year, wagering on golf is becoming very popular there. During these golf contests there is a great deal of side betting on the part of the high rollers. If you cannot get anyone for a side bet, the sports books will accommodate you as long as you are willing to accept their price line or odds. Las Vegas sports books make their own price lines on the golfers and a couple will accept bets up to $5,000. A word of warning: If you *must* make a side bet—and we do not recommend it, make sure you know the party and make sure the bet is properly covered. Watch out for chiselers.

At one time prize fights offered plenty of action to gamblers. But, because of the decline of boxing in the United States, only championship fights are generally handled by the sports books in Las Vegas. And when a fighter is more than a 4 to 1 favorite, they will usually refuse to take wagers on the underdog. At the prize fights held at the Silver Slipper, Fremont, and the Convention Center during the year, side bets are quite frequent.

Actually, at all Las Vegas sporting events, and there are plenty— car races of all types, bowling tournaments, rodeos, basketball games, hockey, etc.—*legal* betting can usually be found if you wish to make side bets. Some of the sports books even offer a line, or odds, on these events. While not a sporting event—or at least it is not recognized as one—you can legally bet on all elections, except for those held in the State of Nevada, in Las Vegas.

Appendix A

♠

Glossary of Gambling Terms

ACE. (1) The 1-spot on a dice. (2) The highest ranking card in poker and some other card games. (3) The lowest ranking card —1—in Pan and Baccarat. (4) In Blackjack, it can be counted as two different numerical totals, either 1 or 11.

ACROSS THE BOARD. Horse race term for placing a win, place and show bet. "Six dollars *across the board* on Spoon Bait in the seventh at Aqueduct."

ACTION. A game, a bet or bets.

AFRICAN DOMINOES. A slang expression for dice.

AHEAD. Winning over and above your original investment.

ALL OUT. Giving it everything in an effort to win.

ALSO RAN. A horse which has finished out of the money.

ANTE. A mandatory bet in Poker and Pan, usually one chip, made by every player before the start of each hand.

ANY RAFFLE. A bet that three-of-a-kind will appear at the game of Chuck-a-Luck.

BACKBOARD. In Craps, the end of the table farthest from the shooter.

BACK LINE. In Craps layout, the boxes, marked "Don't Pass" and "Don't Come," where flat bets that the dice will not pass (will not win) are made.

BACK-TO-BACK. Two cards in Stud Poker of the same denomination, consisting of the hole card and the first dealt-up card. Same as *wired*.

BANGER. The punch that is used to punch blank Keno tickets. Holes are punched to correspond to the numbers selected from

163

the blower or the cage. The punched tickets are then used to check for winning Keno tickets. The marks on the duplicate tickets show through the holes and the winning numbers may readily be seen.

BANK. Money the casino has on hand to meet your wager or pay off your bet.

BANK CRAPS. The game of Craps as played in Las Vegas where all bets are made against the house.

BANKER. A representative of the casino, generally at the gambling table. Often the dealer is considered the banker since he handles the house money in the game.

BARRED NUMBERS. Either the 2 or the 12, as marked on the Craps-table layout, on which "Don't Pass" or "Don't Come" bets are a standoff if the barred number is thrown on the come-out.

BEEF. The act of complaining or the complaint itself.

BEST BET. (1) A wager in which the house percentage or advantage is comparatively low. (2) A handicapper's selection to win a horse race.

BET. A wager placed by the player on a gambling game.

BET AGAINST THE HOUSE. (1) To buck a banking game. (2) To bet right at Craps.

BET THE LIMIT. To place a wager that is the most allowed by the casino.

BIG DICK. The point 10 in Craps.

BIG 8. In Craps, a bet in which the player wagers that an 8 will appear on the dice before a 7.

BIG 6. In Craps, a bet in which the player wagers that a 6 will appear on the dice before a 7.

BIRD-CAGE. A Chuck-a-Luck apparatus.

BLACK. At Roulette, a bet that a black will occur instead of red, zero, or double zero, and is paid off at even money.

BLACKJACK. The card game of Twenty-One.

BLIND BET. In Poker, to make a wager or call a wager without looking at one's hand.

BLOWER. The electrical device that agitates the numbered Keno or Bingo balls and pushes them out through the gooseneck to be recorded.

BLUFF. To bet aggressively an inferior hand to drive the others out of a Poker game, thereby winning the pot.

BOOKMAKER. Person who takes race and sports bets. Same as *bookie* or *book*.

BOX. The marked section on the Craps-table layout reserved for the bet described in it.

BOX BET. A one-throw bet in Craps equally divided among the numbers 2, 3, 11 and 12, usually paying off at the rate for the winning number on the amount covering that number.

BOX CARS. In Craps, a count of 6–6 for a total of 12 with a pair of dice.

BOXMAN. The man in charge at the Craps table.

BOX NUMBERS. The numbers 4, 5, 6, 8, 9 and 10 in a Craps-table layout. Same as *place numbers*.

BREAK. A term for what the casino does to a player when it has won all of his money. Also, the player can "break" the house.

BREAKING HAND. Any hand held in Blackjack which can exceed twenty-one with a one-card draw.

BURNED CARD. Topmost card of deck after the dealer's shuffle and cut by player, removed and placed face up against bottom of deck. When dealer is within one card of "burned" card during play, he reshuffles automatically.

BUST. To exceed a total card count of twenty-one during the play of Blackjack.

BUY A BET. A place bet in Craps made at correct odds, on which the player pays a commission of 5 per cent of the short end of the bet for making it. Can be made either for or against any selected point number. Same as *buy a number*.

CAGE. The mechanical device used in many Bingo and Keno games to mix the balls before selection.

CALL. In Poker, to make a wager equalling that of a previous bettor.

CALLING THE TURN. In Faro, the naming in advance of both the winner and the loser in the final turn and making a bet to that effect.

CANOE. A numbered or winning section of a Roulette wheel in which the ball finally comes to rest after the spin.

CARD CASER. A player who counts the cards played during a

Blackjack game in order to bet heavily when certain cards remain in the deck, or have been played from it. Same as *card counter* or *case down player*.

CASE. In Faro, the abacus-type counting board on which a record is kept of the cards used in the deal and whether they won or lost.

CASE BET. An even-money Faro bet on a denomination when three are gone and only one remains in the dealing box, and there is no advantage to the house.

CASE KEEPER. The casino employee who operates the case during the Faro game.

CASE THE DECK. To remember many of the played and exposed cards during the play of Blackjack.

CASH IN. To return chips to the banker for money.

CASINO. A club whose principal business is gambling.

CASINO MANAGER. The person in charge of the casino.

CATCH. Any number drawn that corresponds to a number on a Keno or Bingo ticket.

CAT HOP. The situation in Faro when two cards of the same denomination are among the last three in the dealing box.

CHANCE. The possibility, or probability, you have of winning a bet you make. For instance, the probability that you can correctly predict the result of a coin-toss is 1 out of 2. Chance should not be confused with odds.

CHECK. (1) In Poker, choosing to make no bet and passing the option to the next player, unless a previous bet has been made. (2) A token used for betting purposes in place of money; same as *chip*.

CHECKERS. The men who in Keno and Bingo verify the numbers on the balls removed from the blower or cage against the numbers showing on the illuminated board.

CINCH. In Poker, a sure winning hand.

COLD. In Craps, when the dice are losing much more frequently than passing (winning), they are said to be running "cold."

COLD PLAYER. One who is in the midst of a long losing streak.

COLUMN BET. It is the wager on any one of the sets of twelve vertical numbers on the Roulette layout.

COME BET. In Craps, a wager that the dice will win, made after the shooter has come out on a point. When the bet is made the next roll of the dice is considered the come-out.

COME-OUT. The very first roll of any new series, or the first roll of a come bet.

COMOQUERS. In Pan, three cards of the same rank of different suits or all of the same suit.

COVER. (1) The house acceptance of your wager on the layout. (2) In Poker, to accept a bet by calling with the required amount of chips.

CRAP. In Craps, a score of 2, 3, or 12 with a pair of dice.

CRAP OUT. To throw a crap on the come-out.

CRAPS. The most popular casino game, which is played with a pair of dice.

CREDIT MANAGER. The casino employee who gauges your bankroll as you gamble.

CROSSROADER. Popular term for a cheater.

CROUPIER. A French term for the dealer or casino representative at the table, usually applied to Roulette and Baccarat.

CUT. (1) The division of the deck of cards by a player after a dealer's shuffle. (2) A house charge, taken by the dealer, such as 5 per cent of the money wagered by players at Poker or Baccarat.

DAILY DOUBLE. A separate totalisator pool produced by single ticket bets on two horses running in different races (usually 1st and 2nd). Both horses must win to produce a payoff. Twin daily doubles involve four horses in an extension of the daily double.

DEAD CARD. A card which has already been played or one that cannot be used in play.

DEAD HEAT. When two or more horses' noses touch the finish line at the same time, resulting in a tie.

DEAL. The distribution of the cards to players by the dealer.

DEALER. The man who represents the casino at the gambling table. Many employees such as stickmen, bankers, boxmen, and croupiers come under the general term of "dealer."

DEALING BOX. A wooden container from which the cards are dealt.

DECISION. The final throw in a roll in Craps, resulting in a win, loss, or stand-off on the shooter's line bet. Actually, the term could be considered the *final* action of any casino game.

DECK. The pack of cards.

DESKMEN. In addition to checking the numbers of Keno and Bingo games to determine their validity, these men check pay-offs over a prescribed amount for authenticity.

DEUCE. The equivalent of two.

DO BETTOR. In Craps, a player who bets the Pass Line or Come, thus betting that the dice will pass, or win. Same as a *right bettor* or *front-line bettor*.

DON'T BETTOR. In Craps, a player who bets the Don't Pass Line or the Don't Come, thus betting that the dice will not pass, will not win. Same as a *wrong bettor* or *back-line bettor*.

DON'T COME. A flat bet in Craps that the dice will not pass, made at any time in the roll after the come-out.

DON'T PASS. A flat bet in Craps that the dice will not pass, made immediately before the come-out by the shooter.

DOUBLE DOWN. To increase a bet in Blackjack and take one hit on the hand being played.

DOWN CARD. A card which is dealt face down.

DOZEN BET. A bet on the first, second, or third dozen numbers on the Roulette layout (1 to 12, 13 to 24, or 25 to 36).

DRAG DOWN. Following a bet, either winning or losing, to reduce the size of the next one.

DRAW. To take cards (or a card) from the dealer.

DRAWING DOWN. Removing your winnings from the table and quitting the game.

DRAW POKER. A five-card game in which the dealer gives each player five down cards. After a bet, each player can get as many as three new cards from the dealer in exchange for a like amount of unwanted cards.

DROP BOX. The locked cashbox located at each casino gaming table. All money paid by players for chips is placed in this container through a slot in the table top.

EASY WAY. In Craps, the toss of a number 4, 6, 8, or 10 in any way other than double 2s, 3s, 4s or 5s, which are known as the hard ways.

EIGHTER FROM DECATUR. In Craps, the eight.

EN PRISON. In Roulette, in European casinos, for even money bets the occurrence of a zero causes the bets to be placed *en prison*. On the next spin the winning bets are returned without a payoff, while the losing bets are collected.

ENTRY. When two or more horses owned or trained by the same owner or trainer are entered in the same race, becoming a unit for betting purposes.

EVEN. Odds of 1 to 1; the bet is paid off in an amount equal to the player's bet.

EXPOSED CARD. Any card dealt face up.

FACE CARD. A King, Queen, or Jack.

FARO BANK. The layout for the Faro game. Also the casino that banks the game.

FAST COMPANY. Seasoned or smart gamblers.

FIELD (1) Several horses grouped as one contestant in a race. (2) A space on the Craps layout containing a group of numbers, 2, 3, 4, 9, 10, 11 and 12.

FIELD BET. A wager made that the numbers designated Field on the Craps layout will appear on the next roll of the dice. The bet is paid off at even money, except as otherwise designated, and is lost if any other number appears.

FILL SLIP. A request in writing by the pit boss for more chips from the cashier for a particular table.

FIRST BASE. Position at a Blackjack table which receives the first hand dealt by the dealer.

FIVE-CARD STUD. A Poker game in which every player gets his first card dealt down and the remaining four cards dealt face up on the table.

FLAT BET. A wager in Craps that is paid off at even money.

FLUSH. In Poker, five cards of the same suit in one hand.

FOLD. To turn one's cards over in Stud Poker and drop out of the hand.

FOUR OF A KIND. Four cards of the same denomination in one hand.

FREE ODDS. In Craps, a bet equal in amount to the flat bet can be made at true odds on any Come or Pass Line bet after the number is determined.

FRETS. The separators or partitions dividing the thirty-eight numbers on a Roulette wheel from each other.

FRONT LINE. In Craps, a bet on Come or Pass Line.

FULL HOUSE. In Poker, three of a kind and a pair to compose a hand.

FUTURE BOOK. Bookmakers sometimes list all horses nominated for a stakes race well in advance of the actual running and accept wagers at stipulated odds. Payoffs to winners are made according to those odds, regardless of the eventual totalisator prices. If a horse fails to start for any reason, all bets on that horse are forfeit to the book.

GOOSENECK. The opening in the electrically operated blower or the cage which expels the Bingo or Keno balls. Same as *goose*.

HAND. (1) In Craps, the time lapsed and the throws made from the come-out roll to the decision (either pass or miss-out). (2) One deal in a card game, or the cards held by a player.

HANDICAP RACE. A race in which the weights to be carried by each horse are assigned by the track's racing secretary.

HANDICAPPER. (1) Track official employee who assigns weights to certain horses in a race. (2) A writer working for a newspaper or racing sheet who tries to select probable race winners. Same as *pricemaker*.

HANDLE. Total amount wagered on one or more horse racers.

HARD COMBINATION. A Blackjack hand that does not contain an Ace. Same as *hard total*.

HARD WAY BET. In Craps, a bet that the number in question, 4, 6, 8, or 10, is made with two 2s, 3s, 4s or 5s before a 7 or the particular number in any other combination. Same as *gag bet*.

HIGH LOW. A Poker game in which the player has a choice of betting he has the highest or lowest hand in the game.

HIGH LOW BET. A proposition bet in Craps equally divided between the 2 and 12 occurring on the next roll of the dice.

HIGH ROLLER. A player who bets for large amounts, normally one who has a large bankroll as well.

HIT. A request in Blackjack for another card either verbally or by movement of the player's cards or hands in a prescribed fashion. Same as *hit it*.

HIT THE BACKBOARD. A request that the shooter bounce the dice off the far end of the Craps table.

HOCK. In Faro, the last card in the dealing box.

HOLE CARD. (1) In Blackjack, the dealer's down card. (2) A card dealt down to a player in a game of Stud Poker.

HORSE ROOM. A race-betting room with all the necessary betting equipment and latest racing information.

HOT. Indicating a winning player, or a passing table.

HOUSE. The casino or its operators and owners.

HOUSE LIMIT. The maximum amount set by the casino that can be wagered on any particular bet. Same as *limit*.

HOUSE NUMBERS. In Roulette, the zero and double-zero.

HOUSE PERCENTAGE. The portion the casino expects to win out of all the money that is played at the tables or machines. Same as *house advantage* or *house edge*.

INSIDE TICKET. The original ticket which is filed and kept inside the Keno counter.

INSURANCE. The player's bet that the dealer will get a "natural" 21, made when the dealer's up-card is an Ace.

IN THE HOLE. The hole cards held by the player in Stud Poker.

JACKPOT. The top-money payback of a slot machine.

JOKER. An extra card added to the standard deck of fifty-two.

JUNKET. A trip to Las Vegas in which the sponsoring casino pays the transportation and accommodation. They are normally arranged for clubs of potential high rollers, or for individuals who will risk an amount large enough to justify the expenses involved.

KENO. A game fashioned after the so-called "Chinese lottery."

KENO BOARD. The large illuminated board which flashes the numbers of the balls expelled from the cage or blower.

KENO COUNTER. That area in a Keno lounge where money is collected and paid, tickets duplicated and the game operated.

KENO GIRLS. The girls who circulate through the casino, accepting tickets from players otherwise engaged.

KENO LOUNGE. The part of the casino where Keno is played.

LAST TURN. The last remaining three undealt cards in Faro.

LAY. To bet a greater amount of money against a lesser amount. For example, "I will *lay* two to one that the Packers beat the Bears."

LAYING THE ODDS. Making a bet in Craps on the odds when

your bet is that the point will not be made. You risk more money than what you expect to win.

LAY OFF. Not to bet.

LAYOUT. The section of the gambling table on which the players make their bets.

LET IT RIDE. A phrase to denote that the player is leaving his previous bet, plus winnings, on the table to be wagered a second time.

LINE BET. In Roulette, a wager on six numbers in two rows of three numbers each running across the layout. The payoff is at 5 to 1 odds.

LITTLE JOE. The point 4 in Craps.

LOOKOUT. A casino employee who supervises the Faro game and sees that all bets are correctly made and paid off and that the case is correctly kept.

LOW BET. An even-money wager on the eighteen low numbers (1 to 18) on the Roulette layout.

MARKERS. (1) The crayons or pens used by Keno players to select their combination of numbers for a game. (2) A numbered chip used to keep track of money owed the bank by the player during a game. (3) A disk placed on a numbered space of a layout to indicate the player's bet. (4) An IOU.

MARTINGALE. A system of betting in which the amount of the bet is doubled after a loss.

MELD. In Pan, a set of three or four cards of the same kind or three or more cards of the same suit in sequence.

MISDEAL. A mistake made by the dealer requiring a new distribution of the cards.

MISS-OUT. In Craps, the failure of the dice to pass; a crap thrown on the come-out, or 7 appearing before the point. Same as *miss*.

MORNING LINE. A handicapper's morning guess as to the probable odds on horses that are to run in the afternoon races.

MULTIPLE RACE PROPOSITIONS. Separate totalisator pools are sometimes arranged for single ticket betting on three or more races in an extension of the parlay. For example, a "five-and-nine" pool covers the five races from the fifth through ninth on a single card. The ticket, or tickets, showing the most winners take, or share equally, the payoff pot.

NATURAL. (1) In Craps, a 7 on the first roll, thus a win. (2) In Blackjack, 21 in two cards.

NINETY DAYS. The point 9 in Craps.

NO DICE. Called by the stickman whenever one of the dice is thrown over the side of the table.

ODDS. Expressed numerically, they give the difference or ratio between the chances of an event's happening and not happening.

ODDS ON. A request in Craps that the free odds bets on previous Come bets be working (in action) on a come-out roll. For the roll of a particular point, the payoff on the free odds bet would be made at true odds. For a 7 all free odds bets would be lost.

OFF. The temporary removal of any revocable bet from the action at the Craps table by reversing the pack or putting a "Bet Off" marker on the bet. Same as *odds off*.

OFF NUMBERS. Any of the place numbers in Craps other than the point number the shooter is shooting for.

ONE-ARMED BANDIT. A good description of a slot machine.

ONE-ROLL BET. A proposition bet in Craps that is decided on the next toss of the dice.

OPENER. In Poker, the player who starts the betting.

OPENERS. The cards, usually at least a pair, which allow a player to open the betting in a hand of Draw Poker.

OUTSIDE TICKET. The duplicate Keno ticket which is given the player and is actually his receipt for the game's play.

PAIR. In Poker, two cards of the same value.

PARI-MUTUEL. A term in horse racing meaning "wagering among each other." The public sets the odds under the pari-mutuel system of betting by wagering against each other through the purchase of tickets recorded by the totalisator.

PARLAY. (1) A system of betting in which the player, after a win, risks the whole stake on the next bet. (2) A single wager on two or more horses to win, place or show in two or more races. If one horse finishes in the designated position or better (in the case of place or show bets), the original stake and winnings automatically become a wager on the other horse or horses in the parlay. When one or more horses in a parlay do not start, the player receives the payoff price produced by the horse or horses that run, unless otherwise stipulated.

PASS. (1) A roll or series of rolls in Craps resulting in a winner for the front line bettors. (2) In Poker, the act of not calling a bet; in other words to drop out of a hand.

PASS LINE. The section on a Craps layout betting with the shooter.

PAT. A hand on which the player decides to stand, refusing additional cards. Same as *standing pat*.

PAY LINE. The center line in the window of a slot machine on which the payoff symbols appear.

PAYOFF. The collection of a bet. Same as *pay*.

PERFECTA. The bettor collects when the two horses he wagered on in one race finish exactly in the manner he selected. Same as *exacta*.

PAYOFF ODDS. The odds at which a bet is paid off.

PERCENTAGE. The portion of your bet that the house keeps by paying your winning bets at less than true odds.

PICTURE CARD. A King, Queen, or Jack.

PIT. The area enclosed by the gambling tables, barred to the non-playing public.

PIT BOSS. The man who supervises all the games in the casino. Should any disputes arise over a bet or the rules he is the final arbiter.

PIT GAMES. Blackjack, Craps and Roulette are generally considered pit games.

PLACE BET. (1) A wager made in Craps on one of the box numbers without waiting for a point. (2) A wager on a horse to finish second. Same as *point bet*.

POINT. In Craps, any of the numbers 4, 5, 6, 8, 9, or 10; or one of those six numbers rolled on the come-out. The shooter and the Pass Line bettors win if the number is tossed again before a 7.

POT. An area in the middle of the table where Poker players place their chips when making or calling a bet.

PRESS A BET. A request by the bettor to increase the size of an existing wager.

PROGRESSION BETTING. Increasing the size of bets by a set formula.

PROPOSITION BET. A general term applied to all Craps bets other than Pass, Don't Pass, Come and Don't Come wagers.

PUCK. The indicator which denotes the Craps shooter's point and odds on or off.

PUNTER. In Baccarat, the player who places the largest player bet. It is the punter who plays the player hand.

PUSH. In Blackjack, a tie hand; no payoff is made.

QUARTER BET. A wager on any four numbers making a square on the Roulette layout, paying 8 to 1. Same as *square bet*.

QUINELLA. A separate totalisator pool produced by single ticket bets on two horses running in the same race. Both horses must finish no worse than second to produce a payoff.

RACK. A box partitioned to hold a certain number of chips.

RAIL. The side of the Craps table.

RAISE. In Poker, to increase the amount of the bet by a set amount.

RANK. The denomination of the playing cards.

RED. An even money wager on the eighteen red numbers on the Roulette layout.

REVISED LINE. A racing sheet which prints the latest revised odds. Same as *late line*.

REVOCABLE BET. Any wager which may be withdrawn after it has been made, before a decision is reached on it.

ROLL. In Craps, a toss of the dice.

RUG JOINT. A top-grade casino such as those on the Las Vegas Strip. Same as a *carpet joint*.

SAWDUST JOINT. A casino that caters to small bettors.

SCORE. To win at gambling.

SCRATCH. To withdraw a horse from a race in which it has been entered.

SEE. To call a bet in Poker.

SEVEN-CARD STUD. A Poker game in which the player is dealt four cards up and three cards face down in the hole.

SEVEN OUT. In Craps, the act of throwing a 7 on anything but a come-out roll. The shooter loses the dice which are then passed to the next player.

SHIFT BOSS. A casino executive in charge of the complete shift of casino employees on duty at any given time.

SHILL. A person hired by the house to play at certain games. Same as *game starters*.

SHOE. A device used to hold two or more decks of cards. Same as a *sabot*.

SHOOTER. In Craps, the player tossing the dice.

SHORT END. The lesser amount risk in any bet that is not at even money.

SHOW. The third place finish in a horse race.

SHUFFLE. Rearrangement of the cards before dealing, always done by the dealer.

SIDE GAME. A minor banking game in a large casino.

SINGLE THROW BET. A bet that is decided on one roll of the dice.

SLEEPER. A bet left on the table by a player's forgetfulness.

SMART MONEY. Money bet by those in the know, such as professional gamblers. Supposedly, the smart money is always bet on the winner.

SNAKE EYES. In Craps, the dice number total of two.

SODA. In Faro, the exposed top card in the deck when the full deck is placed in the dealing box. *Soda to hock* is the complete deal, from top to bottom of the deck.

SOFT COMBINATION. A Blackjack hand that contains an Ace.

SOFT 17. In Blackjack a count of 17 which includes an Ace.

SOFT TOTALS. In Blackjack, those totals in which the Ace when counted as 11 cannot be broken.

SPLIT. In Blackjack, the breaking of a pair into two hands, with another bet made on the second hand. Same as *splitting pair*.

SPLIT BET. A wager on two adjacent numbers in Roulette. Payoff is at 17 to 1.

SPLITTING OPENERS. In Poker, to discard one of a pair. Usually to draw one card to a straight or a flush.

STAKES. The chips or money in the game.

STAND. In Blackjack, a decision of the player not to draw additional cards.

STANDOFF. A tie, no decision. The bet remains intact.

STAY. To remain in the Poker game by calling a bet.

STICK. (1) The long hockey-like instrument used by the stick-man to retrieve the dice and return them to the shooter. (2) A casino employee who bets house money and pretends to be a player in order to attract business or stimulate the action.

STICKMAN. The person wielding the stick in Craps.

STIFF. Any hand in Blackjack with a hard count of 12 to 16.

STRAIGHT. A Poker hand of five cards in sequence. A *straight flush* is a hand of five cards of the same suit in sequence. A *royal flush* is a straight flush from the 10 to the Ace.

STRAIGHT BET. A wager on one number of the Roulette layout, paying 35 to 1. Same as *single-number bet*.

STREET BET. A wager covering three numbers across on the Roulette layout, paying 11 to 1.

STUD. A form of Poker in which three or more cards are dealt face up.

SUCKER BET. One that provides the house with a high percentage advantage.

TAKE THE ODDS. In Craps, making a bet on the odds when your wager is that the point will be made. You risk less than what you expect to win.

THIRD BASE. The position at Blackjack table which receives the last hand dealt by the dealer. Same as *anchor man*.

THREE OF A KIND. A Poker hand where three of the cards are of the same value. Same as *triple* in Pan.

THROW. Any roll or toss of the dice in Craps.

TICKETS. The paper slips with the numbers used in a Keno game. These slips are marked by the players and turned in to the dealers for duplication.

TOKE. A tip in the form of chips.

TOTALISATOR. An electronic computer that totals bets in separate but interlocking pools for win, place and show wagers, and determines payoff prices. The tote board flashes odds changes for each horse during the progress of betting; also shows such pertinent information as post-time, time-of-day, overweights when the jockey weighs more than his assigned poundage, jockey and equipment changes, order of finish, payoff amounts, etc.

TURN. Each pair of cards worked in the Faro game, consisting of the loser (which falls alongside the dealing box) and the winner (which remains on top of the deck in the dealing box).

UP CARD. A card which is dealt face up.

VALLE. In Pan, the so-called pay card—3, 5 or 7.

VIGORISH. (1) In Craps, the commission, usually 5 per cent, paid in buying the numbers to receive full odds. (2) At other casino games a commission or fee.

WIN. The position awarded a horse that finishes first in a race.

WINNER. In Faro, the card remaining on top of the deck in the dealing box on each turn.

WORKING. Money or chips laying on the table waiting for a decision to be made.

Appendix B

♠

Bibliography

Adams, Harland B. *The Guide to Legal Gambling*. New York: Citadel Press, 1966.

Bacon, Robert C. *Secrets of Professional Turf Betting*. Hackensack, New Jersey: Wehman Brothers, Inc., 1960.

Baldwin, Roger. *Playing Blackjack to Win: A New Strategy for the Game of 21*. New York: M. Barrows & Co., 1957.

Buck, F. *Horse Race Betting*. New York: Arco Publishing Co., 1962.

Colver, Donald I. *Scientific Blackjack & Complete Casino Guide*. New York: Arco Publishing Co., 1966.

Conklin Les. *Betting Horses to Win*. New York: Citadel Press, 1966.

Crawford, John R. *How to Be a Consistent Winner in the Most Popular Card Games*. Garden City, New York: Doubleday & Co., 1961.

Dana, John. *Blackjack: How to Win*. Las Vegas, Nevada: Coast Publishing Co., 1968.

DaSilva, E. R. and Dorcus, R. M. *Science in Betting*. New York: Harper & Row, 1961.

Goodman, Mike. *How to Win at Cards, Dice, Races and Roulette*. Los Angeles, California: Holloway House Publishing Co., 1963.

Herbert, R. *Bob Herbert's Secrets of Handicapping*. Englewood Cliffs, New Jersey: Prentice-Hall, 1963.

Heulihan, Gerald. *The Key to Winning Odds*. Owings Mills, Maryland: Ottenheimer Publishers, Inc., 1965.

Jacoby, Oswald. *How to Figure the Odds*. Garden City, New York: Doubleday & Co., 1954.

Jacoby, Oswald. *Oswald Jacoby on Gambling*. New York: Hart Publishing Co., 1963.

Jarlson, Gary. *Roulette: How to Win*. Las Vegas, Nevada: Coast Publishing Co., 1965.

King, George. *Horse Racing: How to Win*. Las Vegas, Nevada: Coast Publishing Co., 1965.

Lemmel, Maurice. *Gambling: Nevada Style*. Garden City, New York: Doubleday & Co., 1964.

Levinson, Horace C. *Chance, Luck and Statistics*. New York: Dover Publications, Inc., 1963.

MacDougall, Michael. *MacDougall on Dice and Cards*. New York: Coward-McCann, Inc., 1944.

Markell, Barry M. *Dice: How to Win*. Las Vegas, Nevada: Coast Publishing Co., 1965.

Newman, David. *Esquires' Book of Gambling*. New York: Harper & Row, 1962.

Radner, Sidney H. *Key to Roulette, Blackjack and One-Armed Bandits*. Owings Mills, Maryland: Ottenheimer Publishers, Inc., 1962.

Riddle, Major A. and Hyams, Joe. *The Weekend Gambler's Handbook*. New York: Random House, 1963.

Rouge Et Noir. *Winning at Casino Gaming*. Glen Head, New York: Rouge Et Noir, Inc., 1966.

Scarne, John. *Scarne's Complete Guide to Gambling*. New York: Simon and Schuster, Inc., 1961.

Smith, Harold S. *I Want to Quit Winners*. Englewood Cliffs, New Jersey: Prentice-Hall, 1961.

Steele, Walter. *Bet and Win Horses*. Hackensack, New Jersey: Wehman Brothers, Inc., 1965.

Thorp, Edward O. *Beat the Dealer: A Winning Strategy for the Game of Twenty-One*. New York: Random House, 1962.

Turner, Wallace. *Gambler's Money*. Boston, Massachusetts: Houghton Mifflin Co., 1965.

Weaver, Warren. *Lady Luck: The Theory of Probability*. Garden City, New York: Doubleday & Co., Inc., 1963.

Wilson, Allan N. *The Casino Gambler's Guide*. New York: Harper & Row, 1965.

Wykes, Alan. *The Complete Illustrated Guide to Gambling*. Garden City, New York: Doubleday & Co., Inc., 1964.